Charles Wesley in America

Charles Wesley in America

Georgia, Charleston, Boston

S T Kimbrough Jr.

FOREWORD BY
Ryan Nicholas Danker

☙PICKWICK *Publications* • Eugene, Oregon

CHARLES WESLEY IN AMERICA
Georgia, Charleston, Boston

Copyright © 2020 S T Kimbrough Jr. All rights reserved. Except for brief quotations in critical publications or reviews, no part of this book may be reproduced in any manner without prior written permission from the publisher. Write: Permissions, Wipf and Stock Publishers, 199 W. 8th Ave., Suite 3, Eugene, OR 97401.

Pickwick Publications
An Imprint of Wipf and Stock Publishers
199 W. 8th Ave., Suite 3
Eugene, OR 97401

www.wipfandstock.com

PAPERBACK ISBN: 978-1-7252-7219-4
HARDCOVER ISBN: 978-1-7252-7220-0
EBOOK ISBN: 978-1-7252-7221-7

Cataloguing-in-Publication data:

Names: Kimbrough, S T, Jr., author. | Danker, Ryan Nicholas, foreword.

Title: Charles Wesley in America : Georgia, Charleston, Boston / by S T Kimbrough Jr. ; foreword by Ryan Nicholas Danker.

Description: Eugene, OR: Pickwick Publications, 2020 | Includes bibliographical references and index.

Identifiers: ISBN 978-1-7252-7219-4 (paperback) | ISBN 978-1-7252-7220-0 (hardcover) | ISBN 978-1-7252-7221-7 (ebook)

Subjects: LCSH: Wesley, Charles, 1707–1788 | United States—Church history—18th century | Methodist Church (Great Britain)—Clergy | Methodist Church (Great Britain)—Missions—Georgia—History—18th century | Georgia—Church history—18th century

Classification: BX8495 K55 2020 (print) | BX8495 (ebook)

Anon., "Charles Wesley" [the "lily" portrait], ca. 1735, used with permission of Peter S. Forsaith, the Oxford Centre for Methodism and Church History, Oxford Brookes University, Oxford, UK. The original painting is located at the "New Room" in Bristol, UK.

Manufactured in the U.S.A.   12/07/20

Contents

Foreword by Ryan Nicholas Danker | vii
Abbreviations | xi
Acknowledgments | xiii
Introduction | xv
   The Colonial Background | xv
   Charles Wesley's Arrival | xvii
   Records of Charles Wesley's American Sojourn | xviii
   The Outline of This Study | xix

1. The Georgia Sojourn | 1
   Introduction | 1
   The Locus of Charles Wesley's Georgia Activity | 4
   The Georgia Section of the *MSJ* | 5
      Pastoral and Priestly Duties | 6
      Secretarial and Civil Duties | 8
      Devotional Life and Scriptural Orientation | 9
      Literary Influences | 12
      Shorthand Sections of the Georgia Account of the *MSJ* | 16
      The Oglethorpe Material | 33
      The Sojourn in Savannah | 34
      Persons Whom Charles Wesley Met in Georgia | 36

CONTENTS

> The Brief Sojourn in Charleston | 41
> Out to Sea | 42
> Conclusion | 43
> A Positive Afterthought | 46

2. The Boston Sojourn | 48
   Introduction | 48
   The Boston Religious Context | 50
   The Boston Visit | 54
   > Persons Whom Charles Wesley Met in Boston | 54
   > Experiences and Places | 66
   > Correspondence | 69
   Summary and Evaluation | 75

3. Charles Wesley and Slavery | 81
   Encounter with Slavery in Charleston | 82
   Other Documents Involving Charles Wesley and Slavery | 84
   A Puzzlement | 103

4. Charles Wesley's Response to the Revolutionary War and to the American Colonies | 106
   Charles Wesley's Critique of the War | 106
   Charles Wesley's Critique of the Colonies | 113

Appendix A: List of the Letters from Ancona Robin Robin John and Ephraim Robin John to Charles Wesley and from Elizabeth Johnson regarding these two former African slaves | 117

Appendix B: An Extract from the Depositions of William Floyd, of the City of Bristol, Mariner, *and* Little Ephraim Robin John, and Ancona Robin Robin John, *of* Old Town, Old Calabar, *on the Coast* of Africa | 119

Selected Bibliography | 121
Index of Personal Names | 125
Index of Place Names | 129

Foreword

MORE THAN THREE CENTURIES after his birth, Charles Wesley continues to inspire. I can still remember distinctly a day I spent in London with a student a number of years ago. We got lost, and in our attempt to figure out where we were going we came across Marylebone and its parish church. I knew that Charles Wesley was buried there—he was very insistent that he wanted to be buried in the consecrated ground of his local parish, carried by six clergy of the Church of England—but I did not know exactly where his grave was located. I insisted that we trudge around the building even if it was getting too dark to look for the grave. Having circled the building twice, we still could not find it. So I looked around for adjacent buildings that may have been built since 1788, and sure enough, behind one of them was the obelisk gravestone. I was elated. Here was one of my heroes. But when I looked over at my student, he was nonplussed. A Roman Catholic, he had no idea who Charles Wesley was until I told him that this man had written "Hark, the Herald Angels Sing." With that realization, he lit up like a Christmas tree.

    Scholars continue to discover the man whose lyrical theology has shaped the worldwide evangelical movement, and the hearts of Christians well beyond early Methodism. At the heart of the evangelical movement was an encounter with God, a transformational encounter so radical that it was referred to as a new birth. Charles Wesley was able, primarily through poetry, to put the ineffable into words, even words that could be sung and therefore distinctly remembered.

This man "made for friendship," as his wife Sally described him, is best known for his poetry, most often in the form of hymns. Yet Charles Wesley is a complex figure. He was a churchman through and through, a family man, and devoted husband. The letters between Charles and Sally reveal a beautiful marriage and are reminiscent of the letters of John and Abigail Adams. Charles Wesley's vision for Methodism—one that would eventually diverge from his brother's—was the original intention of the movement, a renewal of the Established Church. But all of this came after his time in America.

Having attended Oxford, Wesley soon made a sojourn to the newly minted colony of Georgia. The American episode—for both Charles and John Wesley—has been one of the most misunderstood periods of early Methodism. Often simply seen as the precursor to the more interesting moments after their evangelical conversions in May of 1738, the value of the American episode is lost, or even misconstrued. This is one of the main reasons why the present volume is so vital.

Charles comes alive in these pages as a young adventurer in his twenties, a missionary, and an administrator. He is moody. He is also very human as is seen in his numerous bouts with ill health, a theme that will continue throughout his entire life. His classical education shows through, even in trying times. And it is in America, as Kimbrough notes, that Wesley first exercised his priestly ministry, celebrating the sacraments and preaching the word of God.

Wesley is also in the midst of controversy from the time he lands in Georgia until the time he departs from Boston. And yet he still holds on to a rosy view of the colonies years later. One of the most vital contributions that Kimbrough makes to Charles Wesley studies is to examine the shorthand material of Wesley's journal, previously avoided or even covered up by scholars wanting to avoid controversial elements in the narrative. Here we see Wesley on full display.

Kimbrough digs deeply into the American narrative, not stopping at the *Manuscript Journals*—vital as they are—but filling in the details of the narrative with letters and historical details about the colonial context, much from primary source materials. He even extends the narrative by examining relationships that would continue after Wesley returned to England. These include his continued encounters with two enslaved men whom Wesley met in Charleston and encountered again in Bristol.

Kimbrough examines Wesley's views of the American Revolution as seen in his secular poetry later in life, revealing not only his allegiance to the Hanoverian dynasty but also his unshakable Tory commitments. Wesley is often remembered by Methodists for his acerbic challenge to his brother's irregular ordinations, yet they need also to see his challenge to the generals of the British forces in America to get a better view of his poetic arsenal.

On a personal note, I'm particularly glad to see further analysis of Wesley in Boston having lived and studied there and published on Charles Wesley in Boston. I still remember—as I sat in the top floor of the Boston Athenaeum—the moment when I realized not only who the doctor mentioned in Wesley's journal was, Nathaniel Williams, but that he was buried about forty feet away! Kimbrough's in-depth analysis of the Boston period expands the narrative even further.

For years, S T Kimbrough Jr. has tirelessly sought to make Charles Wesley known, through publications, analysis of his theology, and also through the publication of little-known portions of Wesley's vast poetic corpus. The *Manuscript Journals*, another project Kimbrough published in 2007 with Kenneth Newport, will serve as the critical edition of Charles Wesley's journal. Kimbrough founded The Charles Wesley Society and served as its first president and director of publicatioins. He has even played Wesley in a superb one-man show titled *Sweet Singer*! It was within the Wesleyan studies world that we first met and I have had the distinct pleasure to learn from S T now as a colleague and friend for many years. The present volume is yet one more addition to his invaluable contribution to the field.

Ryan Nicholas Danker

Associate Professor of Church History and Methodist Studies
Wesley Theological Seminary
President, Charles Wesley Society

Abbreviations

AM	*The Arminian Magazine*
AV	Authorized Version of the Bible, King James Version
CPH	*Collection of Psalms and Hymns.* Edited by John Wesley. Charles-Town: Lewis Timothy, 1737.
HI	*Hymns of Intercession for all Mankind.* N.p., 1759.
JWW	*The Works of John Wesley.*
	Vol. 18 *Journals and Diaries I (1735–1738)*
	Vol. 25 *Letters I (1721–1739).*
MH	*Methodist History*
MSJ	*The Manuscript Journal of the Reverend Charles Wesley, MA.* Edited by S T Kimbrough Jr. and Kenneth G. C. Newport. 2 vols. Nashville: Abingdon, 2008.
MSP	*Manuscript Patriotism*
PCWS	*Proceedings of the Charles Wesley Society*
PW	*The Poetical Works of John and Charles Wesley.* Edited by George Osborn. 13 Vols. London: The Methodist Conference, 1868–1872.

ABBREVIATIONS

Rep. Verse *Representative Verse of Charles Wesley.* Edited by Frank Baker. London: Epworth, 1962.

UP *The Unpublished Poetry of Charles Wesley.* Edited by S T Kimbrough Jr. and Oliver A. Beckerlegge. 3 Vols. Nashville: Abingdon, 1988, 1990, 1992.

Acknowledgments

THE AUTHOR EXPRESSSES DEEP appreciation to the General Commission on Archives and History for permission to publish in revised form material previously published in the journal *Methodist History*, which it publishes. In addition, appreciation is also expressed to The Methodist Archives of The Methodist Church in Great Britain housed at the John Rylands Library in Manchester, UK, for use of quoted material from the letters of the former slaves, Ancona Robin Robin John and Little Ephraim Robin John. Finally, the author is grateful to Charles A. Green for assistance in technical matters and Randy L. Maddox for bibliographical assistance.

Introduction

The Colonial Background

MUCH IS KNOWN ABOUT the Colony of Georgia in the New World to which the Wesley brothers went as missionaries of the Church of England. It was common knowledge that this area was first settled by the Spanish. The first settlement was perhaps near St. Catherine's Island and led by Vásquez de Ayilón (1480–1526). Plagued by illness, death, and division, the settlement was abandoned within a few months.

The Spanish explorer Hernan de Soto (1500–1542) also chronicled his expedition through Georgia in 1540, in which one learns of a number of Native American encounters. Spanish Roman Catholics had also settled on St. Catherine's Island in 1566. The first explorer from England in Georgia was Henry Woodward, who traveled in the 1670s to the heart of the Creek Nation at Chattahoochee Falls. Through the alliance he achieved with the Creeks, they joined forces to drive the Spanish from Georgia.

In 1732 the Colony of Georgia was officially established. It was the thirteenth and final colony of Great Britain. Colonel[1]

---

1. Colonel was Oglethorpe's military rank at the time he went to Georgia. Around the time of the Jacobite Rebellion (1745), during or after, Oglethorpe was given the title of General.

INTRODUCTION

James Oglethorpe had distinguished himself not only as a British officer, but thereafter had also dedicated himself to assisting the poor and marginalized. This served as a basis, at least so it has been thought, for the origin of the official founding of the Colony of Georgia, named after the current King George II. Interestingly, a primary purpose of the colony, however, was to serve as a buffer between the English and Spanish colonies.

Oglethorpe advertised in the London papers seeking to enlist poor people who were to receive free passage to the New World, along with land, supplies, and food for a year. Soon 35 families, a total of 135 persons, were chosen. On November 16, 1732, they set sail from Gravesend on the ship *Anne*. In 1733, they arrived and founded the city of Savannah. Though where they settled was the site of a Yamacraw village, Oglethorpe, with the help of the elderly chief of the Creeks, Tomochichi, negotiated the move of the village. John Musgrove, who owned a nearby trading post and was married to a woman who was part Yamacraw, served as Oglethorpe's interpreter.

Interestingly, the colony was to be governed by a Board of Trustees in London, which declared from the outset that slavery, lawyers, Catholics, and rum were prohibited. Though Oglethorpe, in large measure, envisioned the colony as a haven for the poor from debtors' prisons, it was the prohibition of slavery and respect for the Native American tribes that made the Georgia colony unique. In reality, the first settlers were not poor debtors. Because establishing a new colony would be difficult, settlers with diverse skills had been chosen.

Though John and Charles Wesley hoped to convert Native Americans to Christianity, what they may have known about them before their arrival in Georgia is unknown. Before Europeans arrived in the area known as Georgia, Native Americans had occupied the land for thousands of years. And, as is well known, the incursion of Europeans brought the advent of numerous diseases previously unknown among Native Americans.

While the Creek Nation is the one about whom one reads in Charles's report of Oglethorpe's activities, historically there were

INTRODUCTION

many tribes with a long history in Georgia: Apalachee, Chatot, Cherokee, Chiaha, Chickasaw, Creek, Shawnee, and many more. Charles Wesley's *MSJ* includes a record of some of Oglethorpe's encounters with local tribes.

Charles Wesley's Arrival

When John and Charles Wesley arrived in North America, it had already had more than a century of exploration by European powers: Spain, France, and England. While it was indeed a new frontier, it was a frontier with a history of conflicts among the European countries, as well as with Native Americans. There had been wars and many more were to come. It is against this background that one begins the study of Charles Wesley's record of his time in America. He enters a new world fraught with strife and difficulties. A young, newly ordained priest of the Church of England arrives in America with misgivings about the precarious journey, and even the priesthood, to serve as a missionary and as Oglethorpe's personal secretary. From a letter written to friends back in England while on board the *Simmonds*, just off Tibey Island, on February 5, 1736, one learns of Charles Wesley's dark mood:

> God has brought an unhappy, unthankful wretch hither, through a thousand dangers, to renew his complaints, and loathe the life which has been preserved by a series of miracles. I take the moment of my arrival to inform you of it, because I know you will thank Him, though I cannot. I cannot, for I yet feel myself. In vain have I fled from myself to America; I still groan under the intolerable weight of inherent misery! If I have never yet repented of my undertaking, it is because I could hope for nothing better in England—or Paradise. Go where I will, I carry my Hell about me.[2]

Mood swings are typical of Charles's demeanor, and at the conclusion of the letter one senses a more upbeat young man, as he entreats his friends:

2. Baker, *Charles Wesley as Revealed by His Letters*, 22.

INTRODUCTION

> I cannot follow my own advice, but yet I advise you—Give God your hearts; love Him with all your souls; serve Him with all your strength. . . . Think of nothing else. See nothing else. To love God, and to be beloved of Him, is enough.

Again, fluctuation of Charles's moods is seen almost a month later in the first entry of his *MSJ* on Tuesday, March 9, 1736: "About three in the afternoon, I first set foot on St Simons Island, and immediately my spirit revived. No sooner did I enter upon my ministry than God gave me, like Saul, another heart."[3]

Throughout his stay in the colony, as his *MSJ* reveals, there are constant mood swings between joy and disappointment. This is not only emotional, but linked as well to physical difficulties. This is the Charles Wesley who enters the Colony of Georgia as a missionary and a secretary to James Oglethorpe.

Records of Charles Wesley's American Sojourn

Charles Wesley spent roughly six and one half months in America and about one month on board a ship as it floundered up the east coast from Charleston[4] to Boston. On September 24, the ship docked near Boston for repairs. Twenty-six days later, on October 26, the ship cleared land for its return voyage to England. This book examines the record of Charles's stay in America from March 9, 1736, the day of his arrival on St. Simon's Island in Georgia, and his first recorded entry in his *MSJ*, to October 26, the day of departure from Boston to England.

There are three primary geographical locations treated in what may be referred to as the American section of Wesley's *MSJ*: the Colony of Georgia, Charleston (located in the area that would

---

3. *MSJ* 1:1. The new publication of Charles Wesley's *MSJ* in 2008 greatly enhanced the understanding of his time in America, particularly the shorthand passages. The editors of the *MSJ* are grateful for the assistance of Randy L. Maddox and Richard P. Heitzenrater in the completion of the publication.

4. In the early days of the founding of this colony it was spelled "Charlestown." The spelling of "Charleston" is used throughout this study, except where Wesley used the old spelling.

become South Carolina), and Boston of the Massachusetts Bay Colony. Where possible Wesley's *MSJ* entries have been amplified and/or expanded by his letters written during his stay in the American colonies.

Charles's sojourn in America was formative for the rest of his life. There the seeds were sown that would bear fruit for the remainder of his pastoral and priestly ministries: preaching, counseling, administration of the sacraments, practice of the daily offices, etc. In the American section of his *MSJ* one also sees how Wesley appropriated his classical learning in a keen interpretive process, through many citations of classical literature and their integration into his understanding of life and the practice of the Christian faith.

The shorthand passages of the Georgia period of the *MSJ* are crucial in revealing the truth about false accusations of sexual impropriety that were made against him. Some of these passages were first deciphered and published in 2007.[5] Previous editors of Charles Wesley's *MSJ* material, e.g., Nehemiah Curnock, John Telford, and Elijah Hoole, no doubt found some of this material too sensitive to print, and hence, they left much of it undeciphered, or at least unpublished. These shorthand sections provide an important corrective to historians of Methodism and the Wesleys who have maintained that the Wesley brothers, John and Charles, did not return to England from the American colonies as defeated men. Charles Wesley, as one finds in the full text of the *MSJ*, departed America a beaten man.

Important letters to and from Charles Wesley with information regarding his time in America are also included where pertinent. Especially interesting is his lengthy personal letter written over a few days in October 1737 before the final departure for England.

---

5. See Kimbrough Jr., "Charles Wesley in Georgia."

INTRODUCTION

The Outline of This Study

The first chapter addresses the conflict between Charles Wesley and Governor Oglethorpe, the full explanation of which has remained somewhat enigmatic. One of the recently deciphered shorthand passages, however, sheds new light on the conflict.

In addition, the brief record of Charles Wesley's stay in Charleston, which is rarely cited, is informative for the understanding of his lifelong opposition to slavery.

Charles Wesley's sojourn in Boston is carefully studied in chapter 2, as well as the repertory of persons mentioned in the Boston section of the *MSJ*. They are identified and Charles's association with them explored. One discovers that Wesley was protected by his Bostonian Anglican colleagues from the hotbed of religious tension in Boston among Dissenters, Puritans, Congregationalists, Presbyterians, and Anglicans. In this chapter what perhaps was behind the shielding of Charles Wesley from such tension is examined.

What is one to make of the growing tension in the Massachusetts Bay Colony caused by the gradually emerging anti-British feeling and loyalty to the British crown? Was Charles Wesley influenced at all by the dynamics of this discord in the colony? In the Boston section of Charles Wesley's *MSJ* one gains insight, which aids a response to these questions.

Charles Wesley was shaped by the American experience for the rest of his life in terms of his practice of the pastoral and priestly offices, relationships with others, and issues of social justice, such as slavery. Therefore, the study of the *MSJ* of his American sojourn is absolutely essential to the study and interpretation of the lives of the Wesleys and the emergence of the Methodist movement.

Given the fact that the seeds were sown in Charleston for Charles's lifelong opposition to slavery, chapter 4 examines important correspondence with two of Charles's acquaintances, William and Vincent Perronet. In addition, it addresses encounters and correspondence with former slaves after his return to England. Correspondence from former slaves is a rarity, since so many could not

INTRODUCTION

read and write. Hence, the letters from Ancona Robin Robin-John and Ephraim Robin-John, whom Charles Wesley encounters in Bristol under unusual circumstances, are extremely important.

In chapter 5, the secular poetry Charles left unpublished at his death is explored for his attitudes about the Revolutionary War and the colonies. These poems reveal his severe critique of the brothers, Richard and William Howe, high-ranking officers of the British army in America, whom he blames for losing the war to the colonists. In addition, he has extremely harsh criticism of the British government for its failure to support properly the troops and the British loyalists remaining in the colonies and many who returned to England.

Chapter 1

The Georgia Sojourn[1]

Introduction

CHARLES WESLEY'S VISIT TO America (1735/1736) became formative for the rest of his life. It is important to note, however, that he went to the New World reluctantly. His brother John, already an ordained priest and thirty-two years of age, had made the decision to go to the Colony of Georgia as a missionary with Colonel Oglethorpe, and John persuaded Charles to take Holy Orders in the Church of England and accompany him to America as a missionary. Charles entered the priesthood with great hesitation, and he left England with many reservations. His father had just died, and his eldest brother Samuel was too busy as a schoolmaster to take care of their mother. Nevertheless, Charles consented to enter the priesthood and to be appointed as a missionary to the colony

---

1. All references to Charles Wesley's original manuscript of the Journal are cited as *MSJ* followed by the page numbers. References to the earlier published editions of the Charles's journal by Thomas Jackson (2 vols.) and another by John Telford (1 vol.) are cited respectively as "Jackson" and "Telford" followed by volume and page number. This chapter appeared as "Charles Wesley in Georgia," in *Methodist History* 45 (2007) 77–110. It is herewith revised. The Commission on Archives and History of The United Methodist Church, which publishes *Methodist History*, has granted permission for the use of all portions previously published in the above cited journal.

1

of Georgia and as Oglethorpe's secretary. His mother had said, "Had I twenty sons, I should rejoice that they were all so employed, though I should never see them more."[2]

John Wesley's Journal begins with his departure from Gravesend for North America, while Charles's commences with his arrival in Georgia. While on board the ship the brothers had encountered a band of Moravians with a very deep sense of confidence in Christ, especially in the face of death, and they had hope of discovering the same inner peace. As already noted, Charles's soul was greatly troubled. Nevertheless, he began his ministry in Georgia with hope.

Appointed as a missionary, he was also Secretary of Indian Affairs and Oglethorpe's personal secretary. In addition, he was given the care of some fifty English families. He had hoped to be a missionary to the Native Americans, but that never materialized.

Life in the colony of Georgia provided the young priest, who was twenty-eight years old at the time, the opportunity to lead in worship and prayers, and to perform other pastoral functions such as the administration of the sacraments of the church and pastoral counseling. Nevertheless, almost from the beginning of his four-month stay, there was constant strife in the colony, and he was often in the midst of it. There was tension with the Spanish, whose military had made forays into the Georgia area. There was also a less comfortable climate along the Georgia coastline with its sand flies and sweltering summer heat than that to which Charles was accustomed in England. This was not the common experience of a Westminster schoolboy and an Oxford University graduate.

Worst of all, tensions precipitated by two vindictive women, Mrs. Hawkins and Mrs. Welch, created tension between Wesley and Oglethorpe, the governor of the Georgia colony. Mrs. Hawkins, wife of the local doctor at St. Simon's Island, where Wesley was stationed, was the primary instigator of a scheme to destroy the reputations of both Oglethorpe and Wesley by pitting the two men against each other in the following way. Mrs. Hawkins told Wesley that Oglethorpe had made amorous

---

2. Moore, *Life of the Rev. John Wesley*, 1:234.

approaches towards her and had tried to sleep with her. She then told Oglethorpe that Charles Wesley had made similar overtures to her, not only in the colony but on board the ship *Simmonds* as well. These rumors spread throughout the very small population very quickly. For a time each man believed the truth of the rumors about the other, only to discover in the end that the entire matter was nothing but empty, false accusations.

This conspiracy against Charles Wesley weighed heavily on him, and when he finally made the decision to return to England, he was greatly relieved. Still, from time to time in the future he would reflect on the Georgia experience and think that in a return to the colony he would find true solace.

On September 24, 1735, the Trustees of the Colony of Georgia recorded an "appointment of Charles Wesley, AM, to be secretary for Indian Affairs of Georgia." Just two days later they authorized "a new town in Georgia to be laid out, to be called Frederica." On September 24 Charles was also ordained priest of the Church of England. On October 10 John Wesley was appointed "missionary at Savannah."[3] And on October 14, 1735, Charles and John embarked from Gravesend on the ship *Simmonds*, a two-hundred-ton vessel, commanded by Captain John Cornish, for the New World. On February 5, 1736, the *Simmonds* reached Georgia. On board were John and Charles Wesley, twenty-seven Moravians including Bishop David Nitschmann, the captain, and crew.

Charles spent his first month in Savannah, during which time little is known of his activities, except for some comments in John's records. For example, an entry in John's Journal from February 19 states:

> My brother and I took boat, and, passing by Savannah, went up to pay our first visit in America to the poor heathens. But neither Tomochichi nor Sinauky were at home. Coming back, we waited upon Mr. Causton, the Chief Magistrate of Savannah. From him we went with Mr. Spangenberg to the Moravian brethren. About eleven

---

3. Extracts from the Minutes of the Trustees of the Colony of Georgia in *Historical Collections of Georgia*. All three quotations are on page 16.

we returned to the boat, and came to our ship about four in the morning.⁴

Charles, however, apparently did not begin his *MSJ* until he arrived on St. Simon's Island in March.

The Locus of Charles Wesley's Georgia Activity

From the time of Charles Wesley's arrival on St. Simon's Island most of his activity was located in and around Frederica. He was engaged in pastoral, priestly, and civil duties. As Oglethorpe's personal secretary/scribe, his mobility was significantly limited. For example, he did not travel with Oglethorpe on his expedition to encounter the Spanish. Oglethorpe no doubt felt Charles should be attending to his priestly and civil duties in the governor's absence.

There is a record in the *MSJ* of a journey Charles made to Savannah two months after his arrival on St. Simon's Island. He set out for Savannah on May 11 by boat, though the last five miles were on foot. He records that Mr. Ingham, Mr. Delamotte, and his brother, were surprised by his unexpected visit. Apparently he and John, however, had agreed that Charles would stay in Savannah and assume John's pastoral duties, while the latter traveled to Frederica:

> Wednesday, May 19. According to our agreement, my brother set forward for Frederica, and I took charge of Savannah in his absence. The hardest duty imposed on me was the expounding the lesson morning and evening to one hundred hearers. I was surprised at my own confidence, and acknowledged it not my own. The day was usually divided between visiting my parishioners, considering the lesson, and conversing with Mr. Ingham, Delamotte, and Appee.⁵

There is only one additional paragraph about this stay in Savannah, an entry of May 25, concerning the visit to a young girl

4. *JWW* 18:149–50.
5. *MSJ* 34.

who was terminally ill, which is noted below. From May 19 to May 25 Charles provided no record of his activities in Savannah. On May 28 Charles included the long account of Oglethorpe's expedition, and he was no doubt back in Frederica at this time, most certainly by May 31, when he discussed Oglethorpe's message to him about going to court.

The Georgia Section of the *MSJ*

How may one describe the Georgia account in Charles Wesley's *MSJ*? What is the nature of the document? First of all, this is his personal record for the period from March 9 to July 26, 1737, when he was in the colony of Georgia. Charles's *MSJ* is in actuality a journal of part of his stay in Georgia. Out of a total of 137 days for which he might have recorded his activities, reflections, and reactions, there are existing records of only 56 days. That is slightly more than 40 percent of the total number of days. For March he recorded 17 days, omitting 5 days (his record begins on March 9). For April he recorded 15 days, omitting 15 days. For May he recorded 12 days, omitting 19 days. For June he recorded only 5 days, omitting 25 days. For July he recorded only 7 days, omitting 19 days (he departed Georgia on July 26). Whether there are other records yet to come to light for any of this period remains to be seen.

Not all of the material in the Georgia section of the *MSJ* originated with Charles Wesley. There are two large segments that are long reports from Oglethorpe. The entry of May 9, which also includes May 10, is a lengthy report of Oglethorpe regarding one of his expeditions. Charles writes in the third person about the expeditions. For May 28 there is yet a lengthier entry, which consists of an actual extract of Oglethorpe's letter regarding the expedition. It is written in the first person with quotations marks, hence, it appears to be Oglethorpe's own account.

There is the authentic Charles Wesley material, of course, both in longhand and in shorthand. One might surmise from John Telford's one volume of the *MSJ* that almost all of the shorthand passages have been transcribed and are included within brackets in his edition. That is not the case, however. It would seem that Charles wrote the passages in shorthand to conceal the extremely sensitive content which had to do primarily with the intrigue on the part of Mrs. Hawkins, Mrs. Welch, their husbands, and his strained relationship with Oglethorpe. This theme will be addressed later.

Along with Charles Wesley's responsibilities in Georgia as Secretary for Indian Affairs, he was also Oglethorpe's personal secretary, and the local priest of the Church of England at Frederica. There is considerable information in the Georgia section of the *MSJ* regarding all of these duties, but particularly his practice of the priestly office.

Pastoral and Priestly Duties

On Tuesday, March 9, the day of Charles's arrival in Georgia, he recorded, "I spent the afternoon in conference with my parishioners. (With what trembling ought I to call them mine!) At seven we had evening prayers, in the open air, at which Mr. Oglethorpe was present."

The next morning, March 10, Charles wrote, "Between five and six in the morning read short prayers to a few at the fire, before Mr. Oglethorpe's tent in a hard shower of rain."

These *MSJ* entries on Charles Wesley's first two days in the colony indicate his regular practice of saying the daily offices of Morning and Evening Prayer in a long and short form.

On his second day in Georgia, March 10, he was already engaged in pastoral counseling:

> Toward noon I found an opportunity of talking at the tent-door with Mrs. [Anne] Welch. I laboured to guard her against the care of the world and to give herself to God in the Christian sacrifice; but to no purpose. God was pleased not to add weight to my words; therefore they could make no impression.
>
> After dinner I began talking with Mrs. Germain, about baptizing her child by immersion. She was much

averse to it, though she owned it a strong, healthy child. I then spoke to her husband, who was soon satisfied, and brought her to be so too.[6]

This later changed and Mrs. Germain recanted her consent. During Charles's brief stay in Savannah to relieve his brother John, there is a moving account of his visit to a young girl, who was dying,

> Tuesday, May 25. I visited a girl of fifteen, who lay a-dying of an incurable illness. She had been in that condition for many months, as her parents, some of the best people of the town, informed me. I started at the sight of a breathing corpse. Never was a real corpse half so ghastly. Her groans and screams alone distinguished her from one. They had no intermission; yet was she perfectly sensible, as appeared by her feebly lifting up her eyes when I bad[e] her trust in God, and read the prayers for the *energumens*. We were all in tears. She made signs for me to come again.[7]

On March 11 the *MSJ* states, "At ten this morning I began the full service [Morning Prayer], to about a dozen women whom I had got together; intending to continue it, and only to read a few prayers to the men before they went to work. I also expounded the second lesson with some boldness, as I had a few times before." This is Charles Wesley's first record of his preaching in Georgia.

Worship settings were often improvised, as one might expect in a frontier context. On Sunday, March 14, Wesley wrote, "We had prayers under a great tree." Further, "I preached with boldness, on singleness of intention."[8] On Sunday, March 28, he mentioned that he "went to the storehouse (our tabernacle at present)."

---

6. *MSJ* 2.
7. *MSJ* 34.
8. This was probably his brother John's sermon, which Charles had copied. See Newport, *Sermons of Charles Wesley*, 306–13.

The call to prayer also had a different sound from the church bells of England. The *MSJ* entry of March 25 states, "At five I heard the second drum beat for prayers."[9]

There was also regular administration of the sacrament of Holy Communion, though it was not always well attended; and there was psalm singing. "After spending an hour at the camp in singing such Psalms as suited the occasion, I went to bed in the hut, which was thoroughly wet with today's rain."[10]

Wesley's commitment to the sacrament of baptism, both of infants and adults, is evidenced throughout the *MSJ*. On one of his first days in Georgia he is engaged in conversation with Mrs. Germain about baptizing her child by immersion. While he was not able to get her to remain faithful to her consent to the child's baptism in that manner, Wesley mentions another child baptism at which he officiated.

Already the question of form in worship was surfacing for Charles Wesley in the Georgia setting. It is succinctly put in the following exchange between him and Mr. Oglethorpe on March 26:

> Mr. Oglethorpe, meeting me in the evening, asked when I had prayers? I said, I waited his pleasure. While the people came slowly, "You see, Sir," said I, "they do not lay too great stress on forms." "The reason of that is because others idolize them." I believe few stay for that reason. "I don't know that."[11]

Secretarial and Civil Duties

In addition to his pastoral and priestly responsibilities, we learn from the Georgia account in the *MSJ* of Charles Wesley's secretarial duties for Oglethorpe and of his own civil responsibilities that were related to his appointment as Secretary of Indian Affairs. After his arrival he stated that he was so exhausted from letter

9. *MSJ* 10.
10. *MSJ* 13.
11. *MSJ* 15.

writing for Oglethorpe that he would not spend six days more in the same manner for all of Georgia. Nevertheless, he took his responsibilities seriously and often attended court hearings to be informed properly in matters of law.

His *MSJ* entry for June 16 summarizes well his secular duties.

> This and many foregoing days have been mostly spent in drawing up Bonds, Affidavits, licences and instructions, for the traders; the evenings in writing letters for Mr. Oglethorpe. We seldom parted till midnight. Tonight, at half-hour past twelve, he set out in the scoutboat for Frederica. I went to bed at one, and rose again at four; but found no effect this variety of fatigue had upon my body till some time after.[12]

Devotional Life and Scriptural Orientation

One gains valuable insight from the Georgia section of the *MSJ* into Charles Wesley's own devotional and meditative life. Here he mirrors his own experiences in Scripture, as he reads it privately and in public worship. This foreshadows how, after his conversion in 1738, he later writes hymns and poems based on Scripture.

In this part of the *MSJ* there are a total of twenty-six scriptural citations and references, eight from the Hebrew scriptures (Old Testament) and eighteen from the Greek scriptures (New Testament). Charles sometimes quotes the passages at length, occasionally includes the texts with no references, and sometimes he only gives the reference or a portion of a scriptural passage. Now and then he gives a wrong reference. Often he is, no doubt, quoting from memory and misquotes a text or paraphrases it. For example, in quoting Mark 13:9, which reads "Ye shall be brought before governors and kings for my sake," he wrote, "Ye shall be brought before rulers," etc. (March 25).[13] His quotation

---

12. *MSJ* 43–44.
13. *MSJ* 11.

of 2 Timothy 4:1-3, 5, and 16-18 has a number of differences from the AV (March 26).[14]

Many of the texts to which Wesley refers are those read at Morning and Evening Prayer. Frequently the texts to which he refers speak to him particularly in the midst of the conflicts in which he finds himself embroiled with Mrs. Hawkins, Mrs. Welch, and Mr. Oglethorpe.

Indicative of the strength he draws privately from Scripture is the following portion of his entry for March 28:

> In my walk at noon I was full of heaviness. Complained to God that I had no friend but Him, and even in Him could now find no comfort. Immediately I received power to pray, then opening my Bible read as follows: "Hearken unto me, ye that seek the Lord: look unto the rock whence ye are hewn. . . . Fear ye not the reproach of men, neither be ye afraid of their reviling[s]. . . . Awake, awake . . . flee away.[15] . . . Who art thou, that thou shouldst be afraid of man that shall die; . . . and hast feared continually every day because of the fury of the oppressor?" (Isa 51:1, 7, 9-11, 12-13)[16] After reading this no wonder I found myself renewed in confidence.

Here is a series of his affirmations about the strength drawn from Holy Scripture (the scriptural references for the passages Wesley quotes in the *MSJ* follow his affirmations in parentheses along with the date of the *MSJ* entry):

> Was revived by those words of our Lord (John 16:1-3, 33, March 29).[17]

---

14. *MSJ* 14.

15. These opening words of verse 9, though one word is not clear in the *MSJ* are omitted in Jackson's (1:13) and Telford's (27-28) editions of the *Journal*, and both incorrectly note the sequence of verses from Isaiah 51 as 1, 2, 12, 13. The sequence of verses should be Isaiah 51:1, 7, 9-11, 13.

16. *MSJ* 18.

17. *MSJ* 16-17.

> I find the scripture an inexhaustible fund of comfort (Isa 50:2b, 6–9a, March 30).[18]
>
> I found the encouragement I sought for the day, Psalm 52 (Ps 52:1–4, April 10).[19]
>
> What words could support more our confidence than that following, out of the Psalms for the day? (Ps 56:1–5, April 11).[20]
>
> What freed me at once from all anxiety was a word of Scripture (John 13:36, May 31).[21]

Here we find also one of Charles Wesley's principles of biblical understanding, namely, that the Scriptures appropriate themselves to us where we are in our needs. On April 10, he wrote,

> It were endless to account all that the Scriptures, which have been for so many days adapted to my circumstances, but I cannot pass by the evening's lesson, Hebrews 11. I was ashamed of having well nigh sunk under mine, when I beheld the conflicts of those triumphant sufferers, "of whom the world was not worthy" (Heb 11:38).[22]

One discrepancy in both Jackson's and Telford's editions of the *MSJ* regarding Charles Wesley's quotations from the Book of Psalms must be clarified. On April 10 Wesley speaks of the encouragement he found in the Psalm prescribed for the day, namely Psalm 52, from which he quotes verses 1–3. Jackson and Telford both include the AV quotation of these verses, however, in the *MSJ*, Wesley is clearly quoting from the Psalter of the Book of Common Prayer.

Jackson and Telford make the same mistake for the quotation of Psalm 56:1–5 which Wesley includes "out of the Psalms for the day" on April 11.[23] Again Wesley quotes the Psalter of

18. *MSJ* 17.
19. *MSJ* 20.
20. *MSJ* 20.
21. *MSJ* 42. This is written in shorthand.
22. *MSJ* 20.
23. *MSJ* 20.

the Book of Common Prayer, though not without variants. For "thee" at the end of verse 3, Wesley wrote "the Lord" and he misquotes the end of the Psalm as "land of the living" and it should read "light of the living."

Charles Wesley's regular use of the Psalter from the Book of Common Prayer in the daily offices of Morning and Evening Prayer imbued his speech with its language. Years later when he wrote *Short Hymns on Select Passages of the Holy Scriptures*, a Bible commentary in verse, in the section based on the Psalms he fluctuated between using the psalm texts from the Book of Common Prayer, the AV, and his own translations. A large number of the citations, however, are from the Book of Common Prayer. This is no doubt due to his familiarity with the text through regularly daily usage.

One final comment should be made regarding the veracity of biblical texts included by Jackson and Telford: the biblical text they print is not always the text exactly as recorded by Charles. This has already been noted regarding the Psalters of the AV and the Book of Common Prayer. However, there are other instances. For example, Jackson and Telford include Matthew 10:18–19 for Wesley's record of March 25; however, Wesley only included the first line of verse 18 and quoted it incorrectly, or at least in summarized form.[24]

Literary Influences

As in the case of Charles Wesley's poetry, one finds in the Georgia section of the *MSJ* a number of references to literary sources other than the Bible. He was an avid reader of classical Greek and Latin literature, and he apparently memorized large segments of such literature. Until 2007, these citations in the Georgia section of the *MSJ* had not been identified.

The first Latin quotation is found in his *MSJ* entry for March 28 and reads: *Abiit, erupit, evasit!*[25] "He has gone, he has broken out,

---

24. *MSJ* 11.
25. *MSJ* 16.

he has escaped." This is a citation from Cicero's *In Catilinum Oratio* (Against Cataline) 2.1. Wesley appears to be quoting from memory, as was often his custom, for he omitted "*excessit*" and reversed the order of *evasit* and *erupit*. The original text reads: *Abiit, [excessit], erupit, evasit!* "He has gone, [he has departed], he has escaped, he has broken out." He uses the quotation in reference to the departure of Mr. Ingham, who having left will be spared the grief of the situation with Mrs. Hawkins and Mrs. Welch. He has now escaped from it all, which is no doubt Charles's secret desire.

A second Latin quotation is found in Wesley's record of March 31:

> I begin now to be abused and slighted into an opinion of my own consider-ableness. I could not be more trampled upon, was I a fallen Minister of State. The people have found out that I am in disgrace and all the cry is:
>
> *Curramus praecipites, et*
> *Dum jacit in ripa calcemus Caesaris hostem.*[26]

The words come from Juvenal's *Satires* x.85–86 and may be translated thus: "Let us run headlong (swiftly) and while he lies on the bank, let us trample the enemy of Caesar." Clearly Charles Wesley identified with this excerpt from Juvenal's satirizing, self-deprecating prayers, which, as Harold F. Guite points out, "Samuel Johnson englished and modernized . . . as 'The Vanity of Human Wishes.'"[27] Once again Wesley has probably quoted from memory, hence the errors in his transcription of Juvenal's text. The second line of the quotation should read: *dum jacet in ripa, calcemus Caesaris hostem*. Wesley misspells *jacit* for *jacet*.

A third Latin quotation is found in a comment Wesley makes to Oglethorpe on April 24. As Oglethorpe is about to depart thinking he may fall in battle, Charles recorded:

> He [Oglethorpe] gave me a diamond ring: I took it, and said: "If, as I believe,

26. *MSJ* 18.
27. Correspondence, March 31, 1995.

> *Postremum fato, quo te alloquor, hoc est.*
>
> Hear what you will quickly know to be true, as soon as you are entered upon the separate state. This ring I shall never make use of for myself. I have no worldly hopes. I have renounced the world. Life is bitterness to me. I came hither to lay it down.[28]

This is a quotation from Virgil's *Aeneid*, vi.466. Once again Wesley is no doubt quoting from memory, thus explaining the errors in his text. The original reads: *extremum fato quo te alloquor, hoc est.* The English translation is: This is the last (word), which, on account of faith, I speak to you.[29]

On April 24 there is yet a fourth Latin quotation, which Wesley calls out to Oglethorpe in the boat, after he has run through the woods to catch up with the departing vessel. The boat was stopped and when asked by Oglethorpe whether he wanted anything, Wesley replied, "God be with you. Go forth, *Christo duce, et auspice Christo!*"[30] The English translation is: Christ being your leader, and Christ your aid. Elijah Hoole adds this footnote in his transcription of this account: "Bancroft [*History of America*] says that Oglethorpe's motto, given to him by Charles Wesley, was, 'Nothing is to be despaired of with Christ for leader.'—*Christo duce nil desperandum.*"[31]

A fifth Latin quotation appears in the *MSJ* record of July 25:

> I resigned my secretary's place, in a letter to Mr. Oglethorpe. After prayers he took me aside, and asked me whether all I had said was not summed up in the line he showed me on my letter.
>
> *Magis apta tuis tua dona relinquo.*[32]

---

28. *MSJ* 26–27.
29. W. W. Fortenbaugh, correspondence, November 29, 1994.
30. *MSJ* 27.
31. Hoole, *Oglethorpe and the Wesleys*, 16.
32. *MSJ* 45.

Sir, to yourself your slighted gifts I leave,
Less fit for me to take, than you to give.³³

In this instance Charles has supplied his own translation in the form of a rhymed couplet. The quotation is from the Latin of Horace's *Epistles* (1.vii.43). Once again the errors in the text indicate that he is probably quoting from memory. The original reads: *Atride, magis apta tibi tua dona relinquam*, which may be translated as follows:

> [Son of Atreus,] your gifts are better suited to yourself,
> I shall leave them for you to use.

There are other literary citations in the Georgia section of the *MSJ*. On March 30 in lamenting his mistreatment as the clergyman of Frederica, Wesley quotes from one of the Greek classics: ἀφρήωρ, ἀθέμιτος, ἀνέστιος.³⁴ These three words are from Nestor's speech in Homer's *Iliad* (xi.63–66), when he is trying to diminish tension between Agamemnon and Diomedes; the former wishes to abandon the war and the latter heatedly objects (English translation):

> Clanless, lawless, homeless [is he whose heart is
> set on the icy chill of civil war.]

Wesley is describing his own despondency and loneliness with the words "clanless, lawless, homeless."

The quotation from the *Iliad* is followed in the March 30 *MSJ* entry with the following two sentences:

> Yet are we not hereunto called, ἀστατεῖν, κακοπαθεῖν.
> Even the Son of Man had not where to lay his head!³⁵

These two Greek words mean "to be restless, to be wretched." The infinitives may suggest that this is not a quotation from Greek classical literature. Wesley may be recalling, however, New Testament

33. *MSJ* 45.
34. *MSJ* 17.
35. *MSJ* 17.

usage of the words: ἀστατεῖν in 1 Corinthians 4:11; κάκοπαφεῖν in 2 Timothy 2:9 and James 5:13.

An additional literary citation is recorded by Wesley on July 10. This time, however, he turned to English literature and William Shakespeare:

> I was waked by the news my brother brought us, of Miss Bovey's sudden death. It called up all my sorrow and envy "Ah, poor Ophelia!" was continually in my mind, "I thought thou shouldest have been my Hamlet's wife." Mr. Appee was just set out for Charlestown [on his way to] Holland, intending to return, when he had settled his affairs, and marry her.[36]
>
> But death had quicker wings than love.[37]

Here Charles quotes Shakespeare's *Hamlet*, act V, scene 1. This is once again probably a quotation from memory, as the words "I thought" in the sentence "I thought thou shouldest have been my Hamlet's wife" should be "I hoped."

The line "But death had quicker wings than love" is the final literary quotation found in the Georgia section of the *MSJ*. This is the last line of "Epigram, from the Greek" by Samuel Wesley, Jr., Charles's eldest brother. It is found on page 81 of *Poems on Several Occasions* by Samuel Wesley. Charles often went to his brother's home in Tiverton and copied his poetry and had no doubt read this passage before he went to America and obviously before his brother published the poem in 1736. He may even have had with him in Georgia copies of some of Samuel's poems.

Shorthand Sections of the Georgia Account of the *MSJ*

The are five sections of material in the Georgia period of the *MSJ* written in shorthand by Charles Wesley. They are included in the

---

36. *MSJ* 44.

37. *MSJ* 44. This line is from an "Epigram, from the Greek" by Charles's brother Samuel. See the latter's *Poems on Several Occasions*, 81.

MSJ entries for March 18 (SH1),³⁸ March 21/22 (SH2),³⁹ April 16 (SH3),⁴⁰ April 24 (SH4),⁴¹ and May 31 (SH5).⁴² In each instance the subject matter is very sensitive. I first published the transcriptions of the shorthand sections in entirety in 2007.⁴³ Although the shorthand is omitted by Jackson, he indicates with an asterisk or other symbol where the shorthand sections are located in the *MSJ*. There are, however, two other sources, which have included decipherments of major portions of the shorthand material. They are Elijah Hoole's *Oglethorpe and the Wesleys* (1863) and John Telford's edition of volume 1 of the Journal (1910), which includes some shorthand passages deciphered by Nehemiah Curnock. While Telford included large segments of the shorthand material in his edition of volume 1, he did not include all of them, nor did Hoole. For example, both omit SH1, the shorthand entry for March 18. Where Telford and Hoole include the same shorthand sections, their decipherments are not always identical and Hoole generally exercises more liberty. Indeed, at times he paraphrases or summarizes. Nevertheless, there are occasional sentences transcribed by Hoole that are missing in Telford. For example, for Monday, March 22, Telford omits the sentence about the struggle between Constable Hird and Mrs. Hawkins: "He laid hold of her husband's gun, and she as quickly caught up another."⁴⁴

For April 16 (SH3), Telford omits an entire paragraph that is included by Hoole, however, Hoole's transcription is a summary and does not include many phrases from the shorthand. For this same date two conversational exchanges between Charles Wesley and Mrs. Welch are also not included in Telford, but do appear in Hoole.

38. *MSJ* 4–5.
39. *MSJ* 6–8.
40. *MSJ* 20–26.
41. *MSJ* 27.
42. *MSJ* 40–43.
43. See Kimbrough, "Charles Wesley in Georgia."
44. *MSJ* 8.

Jackson excludes all of Charles Wesley's shorthand record in his edition of the Georgia section of the Journal. It is not important to speculate about why. Clearly the material is extremely sensitive in terms of subject matter, for it has primarily to do with the strife caused by Mrs. Hawkins and Mrs. Welch, who accuse Charles Wesley of dishonorable conduct with them and Wesley's conflict with Oglethorpe. What it is important to observe here is that it is impossible to interpret properly much of the Journal published by Jackson without the transcriptions of the shorthand.

(1) *Shorthand segment 1* (SH1) appears on March 18 in the Georgia account of the *MSJ*. It consists of Mrs. Welch's indictment of Mr. Oglethorpe as wicked, a stranger to religion, having kept a mistress in England, and having solicited her in England. She also maintains that he had the same designs on Mrs. Hawkins. Here one finds the heart of the kind of intrigue campaign which was conducted by these two women. Mrs. Hawkins told Oglethorpe that John Wesley was in love with her and that he had kissed her some thousand times and that he wept at parting from her on the ship. Mrs. Welch then told Charles Wesley that Oglethorpe was jealous of him and had done all that he could to persuade her that he [Charles Wesley] had the same designs on her. Wesley records at the conclusion of the conversation that Mrs. Welch admitted that she loved Oglethorpe.

Here is the full text of SH1, except for a few as yet undecipherable words. The first two paragraphs are Wesley's record of what Mrs. Welch said about Oglethorpe and the final paragraph consists of Wesley's comments. The words "From her" at the conclusion are a sign that Wesley wanted it clearly understood, even in his own shorthand, that these were her words to him, not his own:

> Mr. Oglethorpe is a wicked man and a perfect stranger to righteousness. He kept a mistress in England to my knowledge, and even there solicited me. He forebore while I was sick, pretending he had laid aside all such designs, but resumed them upon my recovery. He would persuade me, righteousness is but a church teaching. Mrs. Hawkins persuaded me he has the same designs,

I fear, with better hopes of success. His gratitude set him against your brother. In regard to this, she has told him, your brother was in love with her, has kissed her a thousand times and wept bitterly in the ship at the thought of parting from her. Mr. Oglethorpe refused a long time to believe it. She is exceedingly jealous of me; fell upon me lately with "Must I have the character of Mr. Oglethorpe's whore to secure you?" She has also used him with the utmost insolence.

"He is extremely jealous of you; having done all he could to persuade me you had the same design upon me which he has. He contrived your going into the other boat with answers to hinder your speaking to me."

She further owned that she loved him and was much grieved at the thought of losing his love. Besides she dreaded the consequence of its being changed into hatred as she would then be entirely exposed to the mercy of a woman of absolute power. I encouraged her to trust in God and only then pressed her to seek for satisfaction in the means of grace. From her.[45]

It is important to note that Charles only begins his *MSJ* on March 9 and already on March 18 he is caught up in the web of intrigue with Mrs. Welch and Mrs. Hawkins. It is clear from this entry that they are also very instrumental in the strained relationship, which develops between Oglethorpe and Charles Wesley. It is understandable that Wesley did not want this kind of information spread about for common consumption; nevertheless, because of the sensitive nature of the situation he wanted to keep an accurate record of all conversations and related events should he need to refer to the information at some future time. The very fact that the shorthand exists down to the present indicates that Wesley himself wanted to preserve a record of what transpired.

As previously indicated there is no decipherment of SH1 in Telford or Hoole. Telford includes the following statement at the point of SH1 in the entry for March 18: "The record of her vile accusations is in shorthand and closes with the words, 'With a brief

---

45. Transcription of Richard P. Heitzenrater; *MSJ* 4–5.

prayer I instructed her to trust in God and persuaded her to seek for satisfaction only in the means of grace. That ended her."[46] The phrase "With a brief prayer" is not in the shorthand.

(2) *Shorthand segment 2* (SH2) is part of the entry for March 21. It includes a note from Dr. Hawkins, who has been confined for firing a gun on Sunday, which was prohibited. He insists that Charles Wesley has been meddling in his affairs and that his patients be cared for. He disputes the authority of confining a surgeon.

In SH2 Wesley explains that he had no role in Hawkins's confinement, for the gun was fired while he was preaching and then he administered the sacrament of Holy Communion. Thereafter he went into the woods and did not return until dinner time, about one half hour after Hawkins's confinement.

In SH2 Wesley records that Hawkins maintained that Constable Hermsdorf had alarmed Charles, which he said, however, Hermsdorf denied.

In the concluding passage of SH2 Hawkins inquires of Wesley why he did not tell the constable he had no business in confining him. Wesley adds that going home he was informed of what Mrs. Hawkins's husband was saying about John and himself. The three sentences that follow were not included in Telford's transcription of this segment of shorthand. "Hawkins, seeing me from the guardroom walking with his maid between the two rows of houses, had said, 'There goes the parson with his whore. I myself saw her and him were under the bushes.' Modest Mrs. Hawkins added, 'upon the ground.'" Is the reference here to Mrs. Hawkins or Mrs. Welch? Could the reading be: "There goes the parson with his whore." "I saw him myself here in the residence besides," Mrs Hawkins added, 'upon the ground.'" It is very clear why such a sensitive matter was preserved by Charles Wesley in shorthand.

SH2 continues with a long shorthand passage for March 22. This is Charles Wesley's record of what happened that day. While he was attempting to convince Mrs. Welch not to be concerned with the disturbance, Mrs. Hawkins cried out, "Murder," and walked away. Wesley recorded that he then learned that Mrs. Welch

---

46. Telford, 12.

had joined Mrs. Hawkins in making accusations against him. He then describes an incident between Constable Haydon and Mrs. Hawkins. The former forbade her to enter the camp. She apparently was carrying some bottles and Haydon said that he would carry them. When he held up his arms to prevent her entry into the camp, she broke one of the bottles over his head. Haydon then "caught her in his arms" and she continued to hit him and scream, "Murder." Then Dr. Hawkins came up and hit the constable. Haydon threw Hawkins to the ground and "set his foot upon him, and said if he resisted he would run his bayonet into him."

Meanwhile Thomas Hird, another constable, constrained Mrs. Hawkins, "who broke the other bottle on his head." Then Mr. Welch came up to get into the fray, and yet another constable, Davison, warned him to stay out of the camp. "Nevertheless he ran upon him, took the gun out of his hand, and struck him with all his might on his sides and face; till Haydon interposed and parted them. Welch then ran and gave the doctor [Hawkins] a bayonet, which was immediately taken from him. Mrs. Hawkins cried out continually against the parsons, and swore revenge against my brother and me."

That afternoon Charles Wesley visited Mrs. Welch and wanted to talk with her about the way she had been treating him but thought better of it. When he saw how angry she was, Charles then inquired whether he could do anything for her or her husband, who was now confined. But she railed at him and he left.

One final incident of that day involving Mrs. Hawkins is included in SH2. Mr. Hird followed Mrs. Hawkins to her house and asked her "to return quietly to her husband and trouble the public peace no longer. Upon no greater provocation than this, she snatched up an iron pistol and offered to strike him." The next sentence is not included in Telford's transcription of this passage: "He laid hold of her husband's gun, and she as quickly caught up another. She presented it, but was seized before she could discharge it. The pistol, gun, and other arms were now taken from her, and she put in a guard of two sentinels."⁴⁷ This concludes the second major shorthand segment or SH2.

When read against the background of the fully deciphered shorthand passage for March 22, the concluding entry in longhand script for that day takes on a radically different meaning:

> Faint and weary with the day's fatigue, I found my want of true holiness, and begged God to give me comfort from his word. I then read, the evening lesson, "But thou, O man of God, flee these things; and follow after righteousness, godliness, faith, lay hold on eternal life, wherefore unto thou art called, and hast professed a good profession before many witnesses" [1 Tim 6:11, 12]. Before prayers I took a walk with Mr. Ingham, who was surprised I should not think innocence a sufficient protection. I had not indeed acquainted him with what M. W. had told me. At night I was forced to exchange my usual bed, the ground, for a chest, being almost speechless through a violent cold.⁴⁸

Consider how enlightened this concluding longhand passage is by SH2. Jackson, as has been noted, omits SH2 and includes no entry whatsoever for March 22. He concludes March 21 with the longhand passage just quoted, which is clearly an entry for March 22 in the *MSJ*. It is preceded in Jackson's edition with the sentence: "In the evening hour of retirement I resigned myself to God, in my brother's prayer for conformity to a suffering Saviour."⁴⁹ Without SH2 Charles's comment about being "faint and weary with the day's fatigue" is only a general observation. However, read against the background of SH2, one understands why he was so weary and tired and why he found such comfort in the words "flee these things." With SH2 we also have an idea of what it is that he has shared with Mr. Ingham that Mrs. Welch had told him.⁵⁰

47. *MSJ* 8.
48. *MSJ* 8.
49. Jackson, 1:5.
50. On March 22, 1736, John Wesley wrote a letter to Charles in which he made a comment in Greek about either Mrs. Beata Hawkins or Mrs. Anne Welch. Μὴ γένοιτο, ἵνα οὕτω πάλιν ἁμαρτάνῃ. Γρηγόρει, φυλάσσου, ὡς μάλιστα

(3) *Shorthand Segment 3* (SH3) is found in the Georgia section of the *MSJ* in Wesley's entry of April 16. It is the record of a conversation between Oglethorpe, Charles Wesley, and Mrs. Welch, which continues on April 17. Much of this section is included in Telford's edition, but some very significant portions are omitted.

Charles Wesley's relationship to Oglethorpe became strained, much to Charles Wesley's puzzlement. In SH3 Wesley writes down the conversation in which the truth surfaces as to the origin of the strife between the two men. The conversation takes place within the confines of Olgethorpe's tent. Charles Wesley has gone to him to request "some little things I wanted." Oglethorpe takes the opportunity to bear his soul to Wesley in the matter. He explains that his religion does not consist in long prayers "but in forgiving injuries."

It is the section of SH3 that Telford omits which gets to the heart of the matter. Here Oglethorpe explains:

> Many judge of others' barren hearts. At my landing here, one told me you had confined Welch that you might have an opportunity with his wife, but I silenced [him], and told him that was just as he would have done himself. I believed you guilty of the meeting and disturbance, because of your consequent shyness. I forbade you the use of my things without first speaking to me, lest others should use your name to justify the abuse of my goods. You cannot deny the charge of scandalising me, for you wrote your brother an account of it. I thought you would have been an help and a relief to me. I shall still continue my beneficence to Mrs Hawkins, for it is needless trying to ward off scandal. I refused on

---

δύνῃ. Γράφε μοι, πῶς με δεῃ γράφειν, πρὸς αὐτήν. "God forbid that she should again miss the mark in like manner. Watch over her, take care of her as much as possible. Write me how I ought to write to her." (*JWW* 25:454n5). He adds further in Greek: Κινδυνεύω πᾶσαν ὥραν δύω ἢ τρεῖς εἰσι γυναῖκες, νεώτεραι, ἀστεῖαι, φοβούμεναι τὸν Θεόν. Προσεύχου, ἵνα μήτινα αὐτῶν γινώσκω κατὰ σάρκα. "I am in danger every hour [see 1 Cor 15:30]. There are two or three God-fearing refined young women. Pray that I know none of them after the flesh" (*JWW* 25:454n6).

this account to take a poor woman into my ship and she was almost lost by going on Thomas's.⁵¹

SH3 is included in Hoole's *Oglethorpe and the Wesleys in America*, but as I have already indicated, it is a summary and not an accurate decipherment of the shorthand.

Unquestionably Oglethorpe believed that Charles Wesley had confined Mr. Welch in order to have "an opportunity with his wife." Oglethorpe silenced the person who reported this to him and cautioned the individual that "he was judging as he would have done himself." It was Charles Wesley's shyness, however, which convinced Oglethorpe of his guilt. Oglethorpe maintained that Charles could not deny the charge of scandalizing him, since he had written to his brother about it. Oglethorpe also explains that his relationship with Mrs. Hawkins is "endless trying to ward off scandal."

Charles Wesley absolutely denies the whole charge and says he has checked any reports he has received and would have shared them with Oglethorpe, if he had continued in his favor. That the source of all the differences was Mrs. Hawkins is apparently the opinion of Oglethorpe and Wesley. The conversation concluded with Oglethorpe promising Wesley that he would be the same to him as he had been before all this happened.

The next part of SH3 concerns conversations with Mrs. Welch. She had sent for John Wesley, but he was engaged with Oglethorpe, so Charles Wesley went to her. He found her extremely afraid. She accused Charles Wesley of betraying her. Wesley replied, "Be not imposed upon, your betraying me shall never make me betray you."⁵² She was afraid John Wesley was going to betray her to Oglethorpe.

Telford's edition of SH3 omits a series of extremely important sentences after the sentence—"No, my brother is a Christian; I am so much of one to prefer any sufferings to breach of promise"—and before the following sentence—"At ten I related this conversation to

---

51. *MSJ* 22. "Thomas's" is a reference to Captain Thomas's ship.
52. *MSJ* 25.

my brother." These sentences, however, are deciphered and included by Hoole,[53] and they shed further light on the sensitive nature of the entire affair and the complexity of the intrigue:

> [**Mrs. Welch:**] He [Mr. Oglethorpe] came to me just now, and in a transport of anger said, "So, Madam, you have been so wise as to tell Charles Wesley of your affair. It is nothing to me, but you have exposed yourself for ever." I answered, "If Charles Wesley told you so, he is the greatest villain upon earth; and denied it to the last. I did tell them, indeed, that it was you [who] informed me of his affair with Mrs. Hawkins." He denied his having any regard for her, and said he preferred an hour of my company to a week of hers. I am almost distracted at the thought of his knowing I told you.
>
> [**C. Wesley:**] Be not troubled. You are entirely safe on this head.
>
> [**Mrs. Welch:**] If you have really said anything, he is the greatest villain upon earth. I hear him now. He is falling upon your brother. He will get it out of him.
>
> [**C. Wesley:**] It is impossible. My brother put his life in his hand by speaking to him about Mrs Hawkins.
>
> [**Mrs. Welch:**] Pray, send your brother to me immediately.
>
> [**C. Wesley:**] I will.[54]

In summary, Mrs. Welch told Charles Wesley that Oglethorpe told her in anger that Wesley had told him that she told Wesley of Oglethorpe's and Mrs. Welch's affair. Mrs. Welch told Oglethorpe that if Charles Wesley said that, he is "the greatest villain upon earth" and denied it. Mrs. Welch said she told Oglethorpe that Charles Wesley had told her of Oglethorpe's affair with Mrs. Hawkins. Oglethorpe denied to Mrs. Welch "having any regard for her" [Mrs. Hawkins].

---

53. *MSJ* 23. See Hoole, *Oglethorpe and the Wesleys in America*, 20–21.
54. *MSJ* 23.

Charles Wesley tried to comfort Mrs. Welch, to whom he said, "Be not troubled." Mrs. Welch replied that if Charles Wesley "really said anything" then Oglethorpe "is the greatest villain upon earth." Then she told Charles Wesley she was afraid John Wesley would betray her to Oglethorpe and asked Charles to send John to her immediately.

In the lengthy shorthand section, which is included by both Telford and Hoole, though not identically, Charles Wesley said he received a "surprising account of Mr. Oglethorpe" from John Wesley and said, "Who knows but he [Oglethorpe] may be innocent?"

On April 17 the plot thickened. Charles Wesley called on Mrs. Welch, and she reported that the previous night Oglethorpe had accused her of having told Charles and John Wesley that she was in love with Oglethorpe. Mrs. Welch said she told Oglethorpe, "he was all made up of art."[55]

Charles Wesley then said openly, "Mrs. Welch, you have deeply injured me," and told her that she had

> turned my best friend into an enemy for life. When in the openness of my heart I warned you against that very woman [Mrs. Hawkins], how could you go immediately and betray me to her? Why would you even invent falsehoods to hurt me, and say to her and Mr. Oglethorpe that I raised the report about them? Did I deserve this at your hands? Was this gratitude?[56]

As SH3 continues, Mrs. Welch relents, repents, and explains that she was out of her senses to do such a thing. She acknowledges she knew that Charles Wesley was innocent. "I accused you against my conscience of a base design, and have estranged him [Oglethorpe] from you entirely."[57] Mrs. Welch then explained to Charles that Mrs. Hawkins had been constantly inciting her saying, "We must supplant these parsons, and then we shall have Mr. Oglethorpe to ourselves. Do you accuse Charles Wesley to him, and I will accuse

---

55. *MSJ* 24.
56. *MSJ* 24.
57. *MSJ* 25.

the other."[58] She then confided that Mrs. Hawkins's intention was to expose John Wesley to shame.

Charles Wesley then assured Mrs. Welch: "God forgive you as freely as I do. You owe me a public vindication, but my innocence shall surely meet with the fullest vindication from God."[59]

The following section of SH3, which includes very sensitive information regarding Oglethorpe, is omitted by Telford and included by Hoole:[60]

> **Mrs. Welch:** I will unsay all, the first opportunity I have with Mr. Oglethorpe. I know how enraged he is against you. At his landing he accosted me with, "I hear Charles Wesley has secured your husband and I suppose chose to come to bed with you." I denied it with horror, but what shocked me above all was his saying, "Could not you get him into the shadows, then run away screaming out that he had offered you violence? I know he will say it is a false accusation, but leave me to manage him then!" I so dreaded the consequence, that I have had no rest ever since.
>
> **C. Wesley:** But does not your concern arise not from any regard to my anger or damage, but from the fear of losing him?
>
> **Mrs. Welch:** No! For though I love him to distraction, it is as a brother. Even last night I absolutely refused him when he offered to come to bed to me.
>
> **C. Wesley:** "Do you believe a life after this? Do you believe a future judgment? And that the secrets of all hearts shall then be revealed?" As you believe this, tell me, if all you now speak be true.
>
> **Mrs. Welch:** She answered with another solemn oath, "It is."[61]

---

58. *MSJ* 25.
59. *MSJ* 25.
60. Hoole, *Oglethorpe and the Wesleys in America*, 23.
61. Hoole, *Oglethorpe and the Wesleys in America*, 23.

It is interesting indeed that this passage, which does much to vindicate Charles Wesley, has remained unpublished anywhere except in Elijah Hoole's booklet, though not exactly as deciphered above. Why Telford did not include it is a mystery, since Hoole's document was published in 1863.

(4) *Shorthand segment 4* (SH4) appears in the midst of the record of a conversation Oglethorpe conducted with Charles Wesley on April 24, when Oglethorpe thought he was going to his death, as he was departing to encounter the Spaniards. It seems as though Oglethorpe is trying to "set the record straight" with Charles. He said, "You have been deceived, as well as I. I protest my innocence as to the crimes I am charged with; and take myself to be now at liberty to tell you what I thought never to have uttered."[62] This sentence is followed by a brief section in shorthand, which appears in Telford's edition:

> Mrs. Welch had excited in me the first suspicion of you after we were come here. She afterwards told you her own words as if they had been mine. This she confessed both to my brother and me, as likewise that she had falsely accused me to you of making love to her. She was put upon it by Mrs. Hawkins saying, "Let us supplant those parsons and we shall have Mr. Oglethorpe to ourselves."[63]

This confirms the statement made by Mrs. Welch to Charles Wesley that is mentioned in part of SH3.

(5) *Shorthand segment 5* (SH5) is a lengthy part of the entry for May 31, and is once again the record of a conversation between Charles Wesley and Oglethorpe. Most of it is included in Telford's edition, but one sizable segment having to do with Mrs. Welch is omitted, though Hoole includes it. SH5 begins with the statement, which is found in Telford: "Your brother read me his diary, which astonished me to the last degree, and fully convinced me of your innocence. For if Mrs. Welch could so blacken me, she could you."[64] Telford's account then skips the most sensitive

62. *MSJ* 27.
63. *MSJ* 27.
64. *MSJ* 40.

material to the sentence: "I had intended, if she would have stood to her charge, to have sent for you and tried you before all the people, pulled off the mask and punished you with the utmost severity, especially when I heard from your brother of your having defamed me with Mrs. Hawkins."[65] Here is, however, the material that is left out of Telford's edition:

> Accordingly, she came crying to me upon my arrival, with complaints that you had confined her husband, and come to bed to her. I asked her whether she would suffer it. She said, out of fear, and to save her husband's life. From that time I shuddered at the sight of you. 'Twas such a complication of villainy! To make a fool of poor Hermsdorf; to half kill the miserable husband by keeping him three days under a tree; to take this opportunity of ruining his life, and all under the mask of religion! I could not bear you, or suppress my strong antipathy. She told me you was continually soliciting her to walk with you into the woods, and had persecuted her throughout the beach; and had not actually ruined her. I asked whether she would witness this openly against you; she answered, "No, by no means"; she would not be brought in evidence against you; (observing, I suppose, that I did not appear forward enough for it). "But why then," said I, "did you tell it me? You must now be silent and keep it to yourself." "Would," said she, "would you have me continually priest-ridden?"[66]

The continuation of SH5 is essentially a mutual confession between Oglethorpe and Wesley, each explaining to the other why he has misjudged the other. Oglethorpe thought Wesley had defamed him with Mrs. Hawkins and that he was trying to divert inquiries into his own guilt by doing so. Furthermore, Oglethorpe believed essentially, through his many visits and conversations with Mrs. Welch, that Wesley was indeed courting her and had had his spies pursuing him. He was convinced Wesley had been originally sincere in the decision to come to Georgia, but he was so young and

65. *MSJ* 40.
66. *MSJ* 40.

inexperienced, above all especially with women, that he allowed himself to be "encouraged . . . by an artful woman."[67]

Wesley confessed to Olgethorpe that he had believed what Mrs. Welch had said to him about Oglethorpe and thought his character worse than his own. She had told Wesley that she knew three of Oglethorpe's mistresses in London. Wesley was convinced Oglethorpe was not a Christian and intended take his life. He was freed from his anxiety about all this only through the words of John 13:36, "Thou canst not follow me now, but thou shalt follow me hereafter." He appropriated these words to his situation; in other words, he could not follow Christ in Georgia but only afterwards.

Oglethorpe then assured Wesley that he was a Christian and that his faith was the only thing that had prevented him from ending his "miserable life." He further explained that the turning point in his opinion of Wesley, that he was innocent, came in their conversation in his tent and a dream he had after he departed going south to encounter the Spanish. In the dream Wesley had come to him and convinced Oglethorpe of his innocence. He also began to realize the shrewdness of Mrs. Welch in the whole matter. Furthermore, when he had seen how "sad, so pale, and mortified" Wesley was, he realized also how innocent or penitent, or both, Wesley was and knew he must forgive him, as God had forgiven Oglethorpe. Wesley records that Oglethorpe said, "No, I will not only forgive him, but so forgive him as I would God should forgive me; leave him entirely acquitted and satisfied."[68] However, his own pride had prevented him from conveying this to John Wesley.

At the conclusion of the next-to-last paragraph, and Charles's final statement in shorthand, we find a clue to the silence that has reigned about this whole affair:

> **Oglethorpe:** You, I am satisfied, would be tender of the poor unhappy woman, as I was, leaving her full of comfort though, I am determined never to mention any word of all this to her, and desire you would not.

67. *MSJ* 41.
68. *MSJ* 42.

C. Wesley: That I can readily promise, for my intercourse [communication] with her is over. I am no longer obliged to look upon her as one of my charge, and shall never speak to her of this matter. Indeed, my caution in conversing with her did not spring from any fear of these consequences, but from an advice of S. Spangenberg's, 'never to talk with a woman without a witness, or in the face of the sun.' I followed these directions; but did not see the providential reason of it till now.[69]

In a letter of Charles Wesley written from Frederica to John Wesley and dated March 27, Charles refers to the interception of one of his letters to John, which was opened and its contents made public. He stated, "I have not yet complained to Oglethorpe . . . though I trust I shall never either write or speak what I will not justify both to God and man, yet I would not have the secrets of my soul revealed to everyone. For their sakes, therefore, as well as my own I shall write no more, and desire you will not."[70]

In another letter from Charles to John dated May 1, 1736, one receives helpful insight into Charles's mounting frustrations and anxieties during the Georgia sojourn:

> The trial at last is over, but has left me as a man in whom is no strength. I am fully satisfied of Mr. Oglethorpe's innocency, and he of mine; nor can I say which has been traduced most. (God forgive the same wicked instruments of all!) He gave me, when going lately [into the gates of death], an infallible demonstration of his affection and of his virtue. I will, God willing, never forget him for it. To be so obliged by one who had all reason to think me his worst enemy is far more painful to me than the ingratitude of those who had all reason to think me their best friend. I am heartily weary of my fellow-creatures. . . . My increasing abhorrence of this people cleaves so fast to me that I shall never shake it off. Yet while I am constrained to dwell with Mesech I shall labour to make

69. *MSJ* 43.
70. *JWW* 25:454–55.

full proof of my ministry. When a way is made me to escape, escape I shall, for my life, and not look behind.[71]

From the shorthand segments of Charles Wesley's record of the Georgia period in his *MSJ*, one understands clearly the source of his anxiety and frustration during his life and ministry in Georgia. The source of the enmity that developed between him and Oglethorpe is also clarified, as well as how the breach was healed. However, the omission of much of the very sensitive material until now has prevented a full explanation of these matters.

Apparently Charles never received the desired public apology from Mrs. Welch and perhaps it was Oglethorpe's pride once again which prevented him from publicly exonerating Wesley. In any case, while it may be stretching the point to say that Wesley was willing to take a fall for Oglethorpe in all this, it seems that both Oglethorpe and Wesley kept their promise never to mention the affair again.

The presentation of SH1 for the first time in 2007 is absolutely essential to the understanding of the entire matter of intrigue with Mrs. Welch, Mrs. Hawkins, and Mr. Oglethorpe, for it is in SH1 that Wesley records Mrs. Welch's indictment of Oglethorpe, which is one of the primary elements which initiates the misunderstandings.

It appears that we do not have all of the shorthand segments which Charles Wesley wrote during his Georgia sojourn. The Georgia section of the *MSJ* includes an entry for July 1, which reads: "I was at court while the Creek Indians had an audience of Mr. Oglethorpe; which I took down (as several afterwards) in shorthand."[72] We learn of some of Oglethorpe's negotiations with Indians in the long extract from his letter of report to the Trustees of the colony, which Charles included in the record of May 28. To date, however, the other shorthand records mentioned on July 1, 1736, have not been located.

---

71. *JWW* 25:460–61.
72. *MSJ* 44.

The Oglethorpe Material

As indicated at the outset, there are two major passages in the Georgia account of the *MSJ* that have their origin with Mr. Oglethorpe.[73] The first is found in Charles's record of May 9 and is an account of Oglethorpe's expedition from Saturday, May 1, to Saturday, May 8. The entire account has to do with Oglethorpe trying to ascertain whether the Spanish have taken a Major Richards and a Mr. Horton prisoners, "who had carried answers to the Spanish governor's letters." The activity ranges from St. George's Point, a British stronghold, southward to St. Augustine, a Spanish stronghold, and on toward Fort St. Andrews and Amelia Island.

After a tedious search, one of Oglethorpe's men, W. Frazer, located a sole Spaniard in the woods, who had waited four days on the beach for an English vessel. After some maneuvering by the Spanish and English attempting to outwit each other, by May 8 no word had been received about Richards and Horton.

We learn from a later part of the Georgia section of the *MSJ* entry that Oglethorpe "returned from the frontiers" on May 28. It is on this date that Wesley includes the long extract from Oglethorpe's letter to the Trustees of the colony with a report of his expedition. It is a summary of his encounters with the Spanish, no doubt after May 8, the final date of the previous report of the expedition included by Wesley. The activity centers around St. George's Point but covers sea maneuvering from Cumberland Island southward to Fort Frederica and northward to Jekyll's Island. There are negotiating sessions with the Spanish, namely, with Don Ignatio, the Colonel of the Spanish foot soldiers; Don Pedro de Lamberti, the Commander of the Spanish cavalry; the Spanish Commissioners; and a group of Creek Indians, who had been attacked by Pohoia, Chief of the Floridas, at the behest and with the support of the Spaniards.

---

73. For the overall relationship of Oglethorpe and Charles Wesley, especially as regards state and church and their influence on Charles's activities, see Heitzenrater, "Charles Wesley and Oglethorpe in Georgia."

The end of this lengthy saga is that there was no battle between the British and Spanish, negotiations were effective, and the two British gentlemen were released by the Spanish.

The account of Oglethorpe's expedition should be read as one document for the sake of continuity, though the first part is written in the third person by Wesley, and the second part is in the first person, as if dictated by Oglethorpe. What is important is that one has a glimpse into the frontier confrontations of the British and Spanish, the maneuverability of their ships along the coast from St. Augustine in Florida north to Fort Frederica, the location of Spanish and British installations, the relationships of the European settlers and military to the Native Americans, the devious ways in which they misused the Native Americans and pitted them against one another in war, and the nature and function of military and governmental officials on the frontier. No doubt there is little in Wesley's Georgia section of the *MSJ* that is not found elsewhere, and Oglethorpe's own records contain this kind of information.

The two lengthy sections regarding Oglethorpe's expedition, however, are certainly only indirectly related to Charles Wesley's activity, except as Oglethorpe's personal secretary, and in actuality break the continuity of the record keeping of his own activities. He does speak, of course, of the fatigue that results from his extended letter writing for Oglethorpe, and the lengthy section from the letter with the report of the expedition Wesley may well have been written down from Oglethorpe's dictation. He obviously thought the information within it important enough to be retained in his own *MSJ*. Given the excitement and fear in the colony about possible attacks from time to time, and, if seen through Wesley's own eyes within the colony itself, perhaps one can understand why the peaceful solution for the return of the Georgia colonists taken prisoner by the Spanish became a part of his own *MSJ*.

The Sojourn in Savannah

The last part of Charles Wesley's stay in Georgia was in Savannah. On May 12, 1736, he records that at four o'clock he "set out for

Savannah." He went part of the way by boat and four days later, March 16, arrived at Thunderbolt, and walked the last five miles to Savannah. Though his brother John was expecting him at some point, he, Delamotte, and Ingham, whom Charles met upon arrival, were surprised at his early arrival.

Apparently Charles and John had agreed that when the former arrived in Charleston, John would depart for Frederica to assume Charles's parish responsibilities for a brief period. Charles would then assume John's parish responsibilities in Savannah. Charles not only took over John's responsibilities of leading worship, preaching, and visiting the sick; he was committed to fulfill responsibilities as Oglethorpe's secretary, since the Georgia Governor also had arrived in Charleston. Hence, one finds Charles Wesley meeting with traders and the head bailiff, going to court, drawing up bonds, affidavits, licenses, and instructions for the traders. Long hours of letter writing for Governor Oglethorpe ensued which often continued until midnight or after. On June 16, Oglethorpe departed for Frederica, but he returned to Savannah with John Wesley ten days later on June 26.

July 1 finds Charles Wesley in court again with Oglethorpe and at this point in the *MSJ* he includes a long account of Oglethorpe's audience with a delegation of Creek Indians. This is the second major Oglethorpe passage mentioned above that Wesley included.

The remainder of the record in Georgia is quite sketchy. On July 7, he relates an account of swimming/bathing in the Savannah River with Delamotte, who was chased by an alligator but escaped without harm. He notes the untimely death of Miss Bovey on July 10, and on July 21, John informed him that he was to sail in a few days. Four days later, only July 25, Charles resigned as Oglethorpe's secretary and records his conversation with Oglethorpe, in which the governor asks Charles not to inform the Trustees of the Colony of Georgia upon his return to England of the reasons behind his resignation. Oglethorpe was, of course, thinking of protecting himself from incrimination.

The following day, July 26, Charles Wesley left Savannah with his brother John by boat for Charleston where he arrived on July 31, and would spend a little over two months there (May 16 to July 26, 1736, or seventy-two days).

Persons Whom Charles Wesley Met in Georgia

Before turning to Wesley's brief stay in Charleston it is important to review briefly the repertory of persons whom he met in Georgia.

Whom do we encounter in Charles Wesley's Georgia section of the *MSJ*? The discussion thus far has already acquainted us with a number of individuals. They fall into the following categories: (1) fellow passengers on the ship *Simmonds*, (2) military personnel, (3) colonial and governmental officials, (4) individuals who are known only through Charles Wesley's contacts in Georgia, (5) Native Americans, and (6) individuals of historical importance.

(1) We encounter a number of Wesley's fellow passengers from the ship *Simmonds*.

Mr. Samuel Davison, who became a constable in Frederica where he also ran a tavern. He was also the object of ill treatment by Dr. and Mrs. Hawkins and was the constable responsible for investigating the charge against Dr. Hawkins of firing a gun on Sunday. Davison sought to assist Wesley as he was able.

Mr. Charles Delamotte, a friend of the Wesleys, accompanied them to Georgia contrary to the desires of his family. During his stay in America he was an effective schoolmaster. On one occasion during the stressful intrigue and strained relationship between Oglethorpe and Wesley, Charles sent Delamotte to Savannah as an emissary to his brother John. He succeeded in bringing John back to Frederica to assist Charles at the time. When Delamotte later returned to England, he became a Moravian minister.

Dr. and Mrs. Thomas Hawkins. He was the surgeon for Oglethorpe's Regiment and for the general population in the area. In connection with his medical practice he operated a pharmacy. Hawkins also became the first bailiff in the colony, though he did not last long in that position, being removed in 1742. The following year he returned to England. His wife, Beatre, was a constant source of trouble. She was a vicious and violent woman who, according to Charles's account, fired guns at random, cursed, gossiped, and broke bottles over constables' heads at will. Dr. and Mrs. Hawkins were the source of constant strife in the colony.

Captain Johann Christian Adolf von Hermsdorf[4] was a part of the small group of emigrants (Moravians) from Salzburg, who were fleeing Protestant persecution in Germany. Though most of the Moravians who remained behind in Europe were pacifists, the small group which went to Georgia under Hermsdorf's leadership played an important role in defending Frederica. He was apparently a figure of commanding demeanor, as one encounters him throughout the Georgia section of the *MSJ* in such roles as counselor, builder, commander of armed boats for Oglethorpe, and at one point commander of Fort St. George. When Dr. Hawkins was imprisoned, it was Hermsdorf who allowed him to visit his patients.

Mr. Mark and Mrs. Grace Hird. Of them John Wesley recorded on November 16, 1735: "Thomas Hird, and Grace his wife, with their children, Mark, age twenty-one, and Phoebe, about sixteen, who had been educated among the Quakers, were, at their often-repeated desire, and after frequent and careful instruction, received into the Church by Baptism, whereby we gained four more serious and constant communicants."[75] The above discussion has already noted that he was involved in a struggle with Mrs. Hawkins.

Mr. William Horton, a soldier who later became the Magistrate in Frederica, was also a passenger on the *Simmonds*. He apparently was able to see through Mrs. Hawkins to the true nature of her character. The Georgia section of the *MSJ* indicates that after he had left to build a fort, he was apparently taken prisoner in St. Augustine by the Spanish. Charles Wesley's record indicates that he was able later to get a letter to Oglethorpe.

Mr. Benjamin Ingham was a fellow student of the Wesleys at Oxford University and became a part of the Oxford "Methodists" in 1732. He traveled with the Wesleys to America. Ingham was a

---

74. See Schmidt, *John Wesley*, 1:284–85n16.
75. Telford, 285.

close companion of Charles in Georgia and was also deeply influenced by the Moravians. He saw them as the best evidence of primitive Christianity in the eighteenth-century world. This view was reinforced by his later visit to Herrnhut. After his return to England, Ingham began evangelistic work in Yorkshire. Though he placed his work in the societies under Moravian supervision, he soon severed the Moravian connection. Ingham married Lady Margaret Hastings, a sister-in-law of the Countess of Huntingdon. In Georgia, Ingham was a close friend of Charles. They took walks, prayed, and read together. They discussed the difficulties of the colony (and personal ones as well), and he was a confidant of Charles. When the conflict between Charles Wesley and Oglethorpe became extremely tense, Charles sent Ingham to Savannah for his brother John.

Mr. and Mrs. Lawley. The latter appears to have been ill throughout the voyage of the *Simmonds,* perhaps due to a pregnancy. In any case, she became quite agitated toward John Wesley en route to Georgia. This may be part of the cause why Mr. Lawly accused Charles of mutiny and sedition. We learn from the Georgia sectiom of the *MSJ* that Mrs. Lawley unfortunately suffered a miscarriage during March of 1736, after her arrival in Georgia.

Mr. and Mrs. John Welch, also *Simmonds* passengers, settled in Frederica after the voyage. Mr. Welch was a carpenter and a brewer, who made a reputation for himself in Georgia as being lazy, because he did almost nothing to develop his property, even though the couple owned one of the best houses in Frederica. His wife, as the above account has already described in detail, joined in a conspiracy with Mrs. Hawkins to defame Mr. Oglethorpe and the Wesley brothers, John and Charles. She and her husband, like the Hawkins couple, were also a constant source of agitation in the colony, even to the extent of Mr. Welch's attack on a local constable.

(2) We encounter also *military personnel* in Charles's Georgia account. A number of these individuals are found in the excerpt of Oglethorpe's letter, that Wesley includes. *Ensign Delegall* was a British naval officer who according to Oglethorpe

intercepted a Spanish ship at Jekyll's Sound. He was also a fort commander in Georgia.

Oglethorpe's letter mentions three *Spanish military officers*: Don Ignatio, "Colonel of foot," who commanded the Spanish ground troops; Don Pedro de Lamberti, Captain of the Spanish cavalry, "Commander of the Spanish horse" or "troop of horse"; and Don Manuel, Secretary to the Governor (of St. Augustine) and Adjutant of the garrison.

Captain Dempsey, who was ardently opposed to the introduction of slavery in Georgia, was instrumental in negotiating a treaty with the Spanish in St. Augustine. Though he went as an emissary of Oglethorpe under a flag of truce to St. Augustine, the Spanish detained him. Nevertheless, as the Georgia account in the *MSJ* reveals, Dempsey was honorably released and a peace was successfully negotiated. The final sentence from Oglethorpe's letter quoted by Wesley states: "But God be praised, that by His blessing, the diligence of Dempsey, and the prudence of Don Pedro, all bloodshed was avoided."

Captain Ferguson was apparently a naval officer. We know only the following of him from the Georgia section of the *MSJ*: on May 1 he arrived on the scoutboat *Caroline* and brought a report about Major Richards and Mr. Horton, who Ferguson believed had been taken prisoner by the Spanish.

Mr. Germain, whose death is described by John Wesley in his Journal, was apparently a soldier. We know nothing of his military activity and little else, other than that Charles Wesley had secured his consent to baptize his child by immersion. Germain's wife was much opposed to the baptism, but then consented, though she later retracted her consent.

Captain Macintosh was left in command when Oglethorpe went on his expedition to the Spanish.

Lieutenant Moore is another military officer encountered in Oglethorpe's report. Moore was commander of the man-of-war *Hawk* and was also involved in the negotiations with the Spanish.

(3) *Colonial and governmental officials.* Some of these individuals receive little more than a mention in the Georgia part of the *MSJ*.

Mr. *Thomas Causton*, who emigrated to Georgia in 1732, was made chief magistrate of Savannah by Oglethorpe. He was also a storekeeper and an uncle of Sophia Hopkey, with whom John Wesley became entangled. Causton was later charged with theft of public goods and embezzlement of funds belonging to the colony. In October of 1738 he was removed from all official responsibilities by the Board of Trustees of the colony.

Mr. *Dison* was the chaplain of the Independent Company, which funded, in large measure, the Georgia colonial enterprise.

Mr. *Haydon*, mentioned in Charles's entry of March 22, was apparently a constable, who, in the course of giving orders to Mrs. Hawkins not to enter the camp, was struck by her on the head with a bottle.

Mr. *Parker* was the second bailiff in Savannah.

Major *Richards* built a fort near St. Augustine and was reported to have been taken prisoner by the Spanish.

Two members of the Board of Trustees of the colony are also found in Charles Wesley's Georgia account: Mr. Thomas Towers and Mr. James Vernon.

(4) There are some persons in the colony of Georgia whom we know only by name or through some singular occurrence from Charles Wesley's Georgia section of the *MSJ*: Mrs. Colwell, W. Frazer, Mr. Hutchinson, Mr. Lassel, Mrs. Perkins, Mrs. Robinson, Mr. Tackner, and Mrs. Mouse with whom Charles dined at Skidoway Island on his way to Savannah.

(5) In the Georgia account of the *MSJ* we also meet the names of four Native American tribes: Creek, Floridas, Uchees, and Yamacraw (part of the Creek nation). Mention is also made of Tomo Chachi,[76] chief of the Yamacraw tribe, who was said to be about ninety years old in 1734. The Yamacraws were settled some four miles from Savannah. Oglethorpe took Tomo Chachi

---

76. For his portrait, see Marsch, *Die Salzburger Emigranten in Bildern*, plate 137.

and his wife to England in 1734 with the hope that he would become a Christian and a primary link in positive and friendly negotiations with other Native Americans. Pohoia, chief of the Floridas, also appears in the Georgia section of the *MSJ*, as does the chief of the Uchee tribe, though not by name.

(6) Finally, there are some historically important persons mentioned in the Georgia section of the *MSJ*. *Sir Francis Drake*, the English explorer, is mentioned in connection with the remains of a fort he had built on St. George's Point, which Oglethorpe found and repaired. In the April 24 entry, which includes a lengthy quotation from Oglethorpe, *Sir Robert [Walpole]* and *Gascoin* are mentioned, but they have actually no bearing on the interpretation of the *MSJ*, as they are mentioned merely as friends whom Oglethorpe made.

The Brief Sojourn in Charleston

Charles Wesley made his way over land to Charleston (later a part of the state of South Carolina), to board a ship for England. Charles does not provide much information in his *MSJ* about the stay in Charleston, where he remained only twelve days, from July 31 to August 11. There are accounts in the *MSJ* of only three days: July 31 (day of arrival), August 2 and 11 (day of departure). It is the entry of August 2 that is most important. Here he relates his encounter with the horrors of slavery. If he thought that his spirits were at their lowest ebb, he was wrong, for in Charleston the firsthand confrontation with slavery shattered them completely. The three paragraphs of the *MSJ* entry for August 2, in which he records these horrors, are rarely cited, but they are graphic and descriptive of absolutely despicable human behavior. He tells of a master who nailed up one of his negroes by the ears, ordered him to be severely beaten, and then poured scalding water over him so that the poor creature could not stir for some four months afterwards. The description of the mutilation and physical punishment of slaves he labels "horrid cruelties" and the killing of slaves he calls "murder." When one reads Charles's account of his encounter with slavery in Charleston, it is no surprise that he, along with his brother John, opposed it for the rest of his life.

Though quite ill, on August 11, 1736, Charles Wesley boarded the ship for departure to England. There was little wind, however, and after three days of being stuck on a sandbar, on August 17, the ship crossed the sandbar and set out on its voyage.

Out to Sea

Charles's first encounter with the ship's Captain Indivine was an ill omen of troublesome times to come. "The first sight I had of him was upon the cabin floor, stark naked, and dead drunk" (*MSJ* entry of August 11, 1736). The captain constantly drank himself into a stupor and unconsciousness and gave out irresponsible orders, which, if followed, could have cost the crew members and the passengers their lives. As a captain, Indivine was worthless. Under these circumstances there was constant unrest among the crew.

Adding to the strife of these days at sea was Mr. Appee, who showed himself to be dishonest and a man of low morals, in spite of the fact that Wesley had first trusted him. Of his so-called conversion experience, he sarcastically said to Charles, "Why, it was not new a gratification to me to be thought religious, that I found no difficulty in keeping on the mask; and I had got such a knack of going to prayers and sacrament, that I don't know but I should have been actually caught at last."

The conflicts between the captain and the first and second mates, as well as the rest of the crew, heightened. Wesley's *MSJ* attests to this dissension in the record of a conversation between the first mate and the captain. In addition, the crew was fatigued beyond measure from the constant pumping of water to keep the ship afloat, and they could not live on their water allowance and at least one crew member, Benjamin Arnold, was forced to drink his own urine.

No doubt the ship was not seaworthy when it left Charleston, for it began taking on water after only two days at sea. After a little more than a month at sea (August 16 to September 24), the captain reluctantly decided to put in at Boston for repairs. Having endured incredible difficulties and a constant struggle with the captain, the crippled ship finally reached Cape Cod on September 24, and made port at Long Wharf, some eighteen miles from Boston.

Conclusion

The Georgia and Charleston sections of Charles Wesley's *MSJ* are not a careful daily record of Charles's life during his stay in the colony of Georgia and in Charleston. They are rather his sporadic initial attempt to maintain a daily diary of his activities. In actuality it is a record of only 56 of a total of 137 days, the length of his Georgia period, and 3 of the 11 days in Charleston. One uses the word "record" here quite cautiously, for sometimes there is only a sentence for the day, while at other times he includes lengthy discussions of a week's activities, e.g., Oglethorpe's expedition.

In contrast to John Wesley's Journal, Charles's language is terse and to the point. It is neither florid nor verbose. Indeed, the shorthand sections one might describe at times as pithy.

The value of the Georgia section of the *MSJ* is not in its attention to historical detail. Its historical significance lies primarily in the insight it provides into life in the colony of Georgia and into the man Charles Wesley himself at this time in his life. Here is a valuable record of how he began and executed his pastoral and priestly duties as a clergyman of the Church of England on the American frontier. We learn something of the context and content of his pastoral counseling and preaching, as well as how he fulfilled and was frustrated by his religious and civil duties. We discover the scriptural orientation he brought to his daily experience, which is a foreshadowing of his entire ministry and of his vocation as a sacred poet. Once he broke on the scene as a writer of sacred poetry in 1738, the appropriation of the Scriptures to the context of daily life became a hallmark of his poetic genius and hence, his verse.

We encounter in the Georgia section of the *MSJ* Charles's devotion to the daily offices of Morning and Evening Prayer and the sacrament of Holy Communion that become determinative for his lifelong spiritual journey. This devotion evoked the daily study of the Scripture, daily practice of prayer, and daily reading and singing of the Psalms. Even at the risk of formality and routine, Charles never compromised this commitment throughout his ministry.

The Georgia material in the *MSJ* gives us a glimpse of Charles's appropriation of classical learning in his own interpretive process. Alongside Holy Scripture, the words of Homer's *Illiad*, Juvenal's *Satires*, Horace's *Epistles*, Virgil's *Aeneid*, and Shakespeare's *Hamlet* resonate to interpret his moods, daily contexts, and specific occurrences. The couplet paraphrase in English, if it is indeed from Charles, of the line from Horace's *Epistles*, included in Charles's entry for July 25, is one of the few remaining examples of how Charles learned the intricacies of poetic structure, meter, rhyme, etc., namely, by writing English paraphrases of the classical Latin and Greek poets.[77]

The shorthand sections of the Georgia period of the *MSJ* are absolutely essential to understanding the whole of the Georgia material. Indeed, without them one cannot properly comprehend many of the comments made by Charles in the longhand *MSJ*. These sections add greatly to the knowledge of how Charles Wesley handled extremely difficult situations involving accusations against him and others that were false and that were potentially vocationally damaging for life. While he became extremely frustrated and depressed by the blatant and vicious accusations of sexual impropriety made against him by Mrs. Welch and Mrs. Hawkins, as well as against Mr. Oglethorpe, there is no evidence that he responded in any way other than in Christian love, as he could best interpret it. Nonetheless, it is clear that he, like Oglethorpe, made false judgments in the light of all the accusations.

The shorthand sections offer one important corrective to those historians of Methodism and the Wesleys who have tried to sterilize the Georgia experience and say that the Wesley brothers did not return to England extremely frustrated over their "colonial-America" experience. Without question Charles Wesley was a

---

77. See *UP* 1:143.

beaten man. He had had enough! He wanted to leave Georgia. As early as April 25 during his Georgia stay, he wrote,

> Though I expected every hour that the Spaniards would bring us news of Mr. Oglethorpe's death, yet I was insensible of fear and careless of the consequence. But my indifference arose from stupidity rather than faith. There was nothing I cared for in life, and therefore the loss of it appeared a trifle.[78]

His final Georgia entry on Monday, July 26, reads:

> The words which concluded the lesson, and my stay in Georgia, were, "Arise, let us go hence" [John 14:31d]. Accordingly at twelve I took my final leave of Savannah. When the boat put off I was surprised that I felt no more joy in leaving such a scene of sorrows.[79]

Another important contribution of the shorthand sections is that they give clarity to the origin of the conflict between Oglethorpe and Wesley and how it was resolved.

It is perhaps important to note, though it is an argument from silence, that Charles's preoccupation with the conflict with Mrs. Welch, Mrs. Hawkins, and Mr. Oglethorpe so consumed him mentally and emotionally that he may have neglected to record many of his daily concerns and experiences. This may be a major reason for his omission of so many days during the Georgia period.

The repertory of persons encountered in the Georgia section of the *MSJ* offers no great surprises. It illustrates, however, the broad societal spectrum represented in the colony of Georgia. One might have thought there would have been more about the influences of the Moravians on Charles and while there are hints of this, it is certainly found in diminished proportions compared to the period after his return to England. Key relationships are those to Oglethorpe, his brother John, Ingham, Delamotte, and, of course, Mrs. Welch and Mrs. Hawkins. The array of personages added by the Oglethorpe

---

78. *MSJ* 28.
79. *MSJ* 46.

material does add color to the Georgia section of the *MSJ*, but it grows out of Oglethorpe's experience, not that of Charles.

The Georgia material, that is, longhand and shorthand, along with the *MSJ* material from Charleston [SC] just before Charles's return to England, and the brief stay in Boston provide the foundation for understanding much of the direction of Charles's quest for faith up to May 21, 1738, and his ministry from 1738 onward. Having withstood the trials of Georgia he was indeed prepared for a ministry that would be characterized by constant encounter with hardship and conflict.

Interestingly, in reflecting on vocational options before him (including perhaps a return to Georgia) in a letter to John dated October 1–6, 1736, Charles rued, "Georgia alone can give me the solitude I sigh after."[80]

Charles Wesley, however, was crushed by the Georgia and Charleston experiences. On October 6, 1736, Charles wrote to John from Boston: "Μήδεν πίστευε εἰ μὴ χριστιανῷ" (Trust no one if not a Christian). I have been so befouled, abused, and discredited that I can hardly believe, or expect to be believed by anyone."[81]

A Positive Afterthought

One might ask, Did nothing good come out of Charles Wesley's stay in Georgia besides his encounter with the Moravians, an introduction to congregational song, and the formation of a life-long opposition to slavery during his brief stay in Charleston? Those were three primary transforming forces in his life! There is a letter from George Whitefield written from Bethesda, Georgia, on March 21, 1745, which is an interesting addition to the fruit-bearing seed sown by Charles during his Georgia period. It appeared in a pamphlet entitled *A Brief Account of the Rise,*

---

80. *JWW* 25:478.
81. *JWW* 25:479.

Progress, and Present Situation of the Orphan House in Georgia" (1746) by George Whitefield:

> Romans 12:7, "Provide things honest in the sight of all men."
>
> Bethesda, in Georgia, March 21, 1745–1746.
>
> Some have thought that the erecting such a building was on the produce of my own brain; but they are mistaken; for it was first proposed to me by my dear friend, the Rev. Mr. Charles Wesley, who, with his excellency General Oglethorpe, had concerted a scheme for carrying on such a design before I had any thoughts of going abroad myself. It was natural to think that as the Government intended this Province for refuge and support of many of our poor countrymen, that numbers of such adventurers must necessarily be taken off, by being exposed to the hardships which unavoidably attend a new settlement. I thought it, therefore, a noble design in the General to erect a house for fatherless children; and believing such a provision for orphans would be an inducement for many to come over, I fell in with the design, when mentioned to me by my friend, and was resolved, in the strength of God, to prosecute it with all my might.[82]

---

82. White, *Historical Collections of Georgia*, 329n4.

Chapter 2

The Boston Sojourn[1]

Introduction

LITTLE IS KNOWN ABOUT Charles Wesley's sojourn in Boston, except for his own *MSJ* record. There is nothing of Charles Wesley the poet and hymn writer that one associates with his brief respite in Boston, which was an unforeseen part of his 1736 stay in the American colonies. It is enigmatic, since little has been known about how he fit into the Boston religious scene, which was extremely complex at the time, or how he interpreted it.

Charles Wesley remained a total of thirty-two days in Boston. Entries in his *MSJ* are for only twenty-two of those days. On two of the days for which there are no records in the *MSJ*, namely, October 6 and 15, there are extant letters of Charles Wesley to his brother John, which provide useful information. In addition, his *MSJ* entries for October 17, 18, 19, 21, and 25 are amplified by his letters to John on those dates.

---

1. This chapter was published previoiusly as "Charles Wesley in Boston," in *Methodist History* 45 (2007) 111–33. It is herewith revised. The Commission on Archives and History of The United Methodist Church, which publishes *Methodist History* has granted permission for the use of all portions previously published in the above-cited journal.

THE BOSTON SOJOURN

On September 24, the ship made port at Boston's Long Wharf, and Wesley wrote the following in his *MSJ*:

> **Friday, September 24.** Being within sight of the lighthouse, at nine in the morning, the pilot came on board [to] us. At two I gladly obeyed his hasty summons, and went into his boat with the other passengers, bidding an hearty farewell to our wretched ship, and the more wretched captain, who for the last two days had, most happily for us, lain dead drunk on the floor, without sense or motion.
>
> I was at leisure now to contemplate a prospect entirely new, and beautiful beyond all I had ever seen. We sailed smoothly on, in a vast basin, as it seemed, bounded on all sides with small innumerable islands. Some of these were entire rock in height and colour not unlike Dover Cliffs: others steep, and covered with woods. Here and there lay a round hill, entirely clothed with green and all at such equal distances that the passages seemed artificially made to admit the narrow streams between.
>
> Having passed one of these passages, we were presented with a new set of hills and rocks and woods, in endless variety; till we came to the castle, three miles from Boston. From thence we had a full view of the town, stretched out a mile and a half upon the shore, in a semicircle. We landed at Long Wharf, which we walked straight up, having a row of houses on one side, and near two hundred sail of ships on the other. Lodged in a public house. Went to bed at eleven.[2]

One immediately notices a difference in the style of writing in this prose passage from the rest of Charles's *MSJ*. He was a reluctant diary or journal keeper, but at the behest of his brother John attempted to do so. In spite of his poetical gifts, he generally was not given to florid prose; rather his *MSJ* entries tend to be terse and to the point. In the change of style in this passage from his *MSJ*, however, one immediately senses the emotional and psychological release taking place within Charles upon his arrival in Boston, for he has five months of turmoil in Georgia behind him. It should

2. *MSJ* 54–55.

be noted also that only one of the succeeding entries in his *MSJ* (October 2) during the visit to Boston (there are a total of twenty-six between September 24 and October 26), when the repaired ship on which Wesley was returning to England finally moved out of Boston harbor, clear of all land, reflects this same descriptive eloquence of the September 24 entry.

The Boston Religious Context

What was the religious situation in Boston at the time of Wesley's visit? The Massachusetts Bay Colony had been settled in 1630 and dominated at first by Puritan influence. It was not until 1679 that persons living in Boston petitioned the king that they might be permitted to practice religion according to the Church of England. The situation was complicated by the fact that it was not until 1681 that a law prohibiting the keeping of Christmas was repealed. On June 15, 1686, the Church of England was established by law and officially organized in Boston. King's Chapel, the first Anglican Church in the city, was built the same year.

Fifty years later Charles Wesley arrived in Boston. By 1736 two additional Anglican churches had been built—Christ Church (1723), which became known as Old North Church, and Trinity Church (1733). By the time of Wesley's arrival a number of Anglican missions had been established and several clergy of the Church of England assigned to them through the Society for the Propagation of the Gospel in Foreign Parts. All of the work was under the authority of the Bishop of London, who had also established the office of Commissary in Boston with responsibility for oversight of the churches and missions there. The priest holding that position, The Rev. Mr. Roger Price, was also the rector of King's Chapel. The Rev. Dr. Timothy Cutler was the rector of Christ Church.

As Anglicanism had grown in Boston,[3] so had tensions among religious communities. It was a hotbed of religious controversy. In

---

3. Between 1736 (the founding year of King's Chapel in Boston) and 1786, more than sixty Anglican parishes were begun in Connecticut and Massachusetts. See Dudly Tyng, *Massachusetts Episcopalians*.

addition to Puritans, Scots had also settled in New England and Presbyterianism was on the rise. Many Dissenters found their rightful place within a fast growing Congregationalism. Amid all this activity the Church of England was deeply concerned to establish missions in the New World and to win it for Christ and the church. But the missions provoked considerable opposition from the Puritans and other non-adherents to the Church of England. As loyalties to the British crown waned, so did loyalties to the Church of England, for the two were considered mutually interconnected. Here is the voice of protest from the distinguished Congregationalist clergyman Cotton Mather:

> "*Societies for the Propagation of Religion* which, for *Laborers in the Harvest of God,* send forth Men that are *alienated from this Life of God,* and that, instead of Preaching the *more weighty Matters* of the Gospel, Preach up the *lesser Matters* and mere Accidentals of Christianity, and such things as it is not certain that God has ever Instituted,—these do for the most part serve the *Empire of Satan* under the *Banner of our Saviour;* and by these Cheats a vast disservice is done unto the Interest of the Gospel in the World."[4]

Furthermore, nothing could have been more offensive to New England Puritans than the idea of apostolic succession espoused by the Church of England, not only because of mere formalism, but because of adamant opposition to Roman Catholicism through which such descent in Anglicanism was claimed.

A viewpoint openly advocated by Dr. Cutler of Old North Church roused the ire of many. He maintained "that, *ordinarily,* there was no salvation out of the communion of the Episcopal Church; and that none but an episcopally ordained minister could perform any religious offices with validity and effect."[5] There were also a variety of the King's laws in effect at the time which evoked agitation and turmoil. For example, one law stated that those persons living within five miles of an Episcopal Church

---

4. Mather quoted in Foote, *Annals of King's Chapel,* 1:263.
5. Cutler quoted in Foote, *Annals of King's Chapel,* 1:341.

would be exempt from certain taxes. Yet the "Sunday laws" could prevent them from attending church at such distances from their homes. In other instances persons were taken to court for absenting themselves from divine worship and, if found guilty, were required to pay the court costs.

An excerpt from a letter of Mr. John Checkley, a gentleman whom Wesley met on at least four occasions during his Boston visit, to the Bishop of London in 1728, reveals the complexities of the situation:

> There are but few churches (at great distance from each other) in this great country; and the Churchmen being dispersed throughout the whole territory, they are obliged (some of them) to ride 30 or 40 miles to partake of the Holy Sacrament. It is, moreover, usual for the Church people to walk or ride 6, 8, and 10 miles upon the Saturday evening, or very early on the Sunday morning, to the town where the Church of England is settled, and to return home again on the Sunday evening. But if a stop is not put to this first law, they will be obliged to spend the greatest part of the Saturday and Monday in going (for all are not able to keep horses) and riding to church and returning home. But this would be very hard upon the poor people, who are generally husbandmen, etc.[6]

Into these extremely complex religious circumstances came Charles Wesley, a learned young priest and Oxford graduate (BA, 1730; MA, 1733), who did not want to enter the priesthood and who did not come from an aristocratic family. He had been assigned, after a hasty ordination (on one Sunday he was ordained deacon by the Bishop of Oxford and the following Sunday priest by the Bishop of London), to work in the Colony of Georgia, an assignment that differed from that of many other missionaries of the Church of England. He was appointed Secretary of Indian Affairs, as well as Colonel Oglethorpe's personal secretary. In addition, he also served the small congregation at Fort Frederica on St. Simon's Island.

---

6. Checkley quoted in Foote, *Annals of King's Chapel*, 1:452.

THE BOSTON SOJOURN

By the time of Wesley's visit to Boston in 1736, British immigrants had been living and worshiping there for over a hundred years. King's Chapel, built in 1686, already had a fifty-year history. Boston was by no means as physically wild and difficult as the Colony of Georgia had been for him. The latter had been first settled by Oglethorpe in 1733, largely with British folk of desperate fortunes, many of whom had been in debtors' prison, and Protestant exiles from Europe. Wesley arrived in Georgia in May and departed in August. The summer months were very hot, and the sand flies annoyed him. The climate, living conditions, and the people of Boston, however, were much more civil and agreeable to Wesley. Furthermore, there were established churches and congregations of the Church of England in Boston, which he had not experienced in the southern colony, except for small bands of worshipers who gathered under extremely primitive conditions, e.g., under a tree in the outdoors or in a makeshift room in a storehouse.

After having been ordained less than a year and having spent four stormy months in his first assignment, he was returning home quite dejected, and now unexpectedly arrived in Boston. In discussing the subject of "Charles Wesley in Boston" it is important to remember two things in particular: (1) Wesley had not yet broken on the scene as a religious poet; that only took place after his conversion experience of May 21, 1738; he had no notoriety in this regard. (2) Charles Wesley's visit to Boston preceded the existence of The Episcopal Church and the organization of its Diocese of Massachusetts. At the time churches of the Anglican communion were under the authority of the Bishop of London.

The Boston Visit

Persons Whom Charles Wesley Met in Boston[7]

The Rev. Roger Price

Certainly Charles Wesley's arrival in Boston was not anticipated by anyone. There was no prior announcement of his coming, no letter of introduction. Indeed, there was some initial disbelief that he was even a priest of the Church of England. On his first morning in Boston, September 25, Wesley went straight to the most high-ranking official of the Church of England resident there, The Rev. Roger Price, the Commissary of the Bishop of London. Price was born December 6, 1696, the eldest son of The Rev. William and Elizabeth Price, and was educated at Oxford where he received the BA degree from Balliol College in 1717.

Here is Charles's complete *MSJ* entry for September 25, regarding his first meeting with Price:

> Called several times at Mr. Price, the commissary's, before I found him at home. At first he looked as not believing me to be a clergyman (my ship-clothes not being the best credentials). But when I returned in my habit (Dr. [Timothy] Cutler having met him meantime, and informed him of me), he received me very cordially, and pressed me to live with him while I stayed in Boston.[8]

What possibly could have been Wesley's expectations in calling on the Commissary? First and foremost, he probably felt it his duty, as he himself was under the authority of the Bishop of London, who had jurisdiction in North America and was hence Wesley's bishop. While being an ordained clergy person would unquestionably have given him some status of importance in the British colonies, nevertheless, unless there were some official communiques available to Church of England clergy, which informed them of the current missionary assignments for North America (and that is entirely

---

7. See *Classified Digest*.
8. *MSJ* 1:55.

possible) the Boston clergy probably had little or no information about Charles. Nevertheless, to have been so cordially received by The Rev. Roger Price, the Commissary of the Bishop of London, and invited to stay in his home, indicates that the Commissary could have had some information about Charles, other than The Rev. Dr. Cutler's words of encouragement, whom Charles apparently met first upon arrival in Boston.

The Rev. Dr. Timothy Cutler

It is extremely interesting that just two days after his arrival in Boston this unknown, inexperienced young priest was invited by Dr. Timothy Cutler, rector of Old North Church (Christ Church), to preach in the morning at the church and in the afternoon by The Rev. Price to preach at his parish church, King's Chapel.

Who were these persons first to receive Charles Wesley in Boston? The Rev. Dr. Timothy Cutler was the first rector of Old North Church. He conducted the first service of worship in the church on December 29, 1723, just after the completion of the building. Cutler was born in 1683 in Charleston and was the son of Major John Cutler. In 1701 he graduated from Harvard College and on January 11, 1710, he was ordained and installed as the pastor of a Congregational church in Stratford, Connecticut. Cutler became known for his excellent preaching, for which he was invited to preach before the General Assembly of Connecticut in October of 1719. In March of the same year he had become rector of Yale College.

He became a convert to Anglicanism, however, and went to England for his ordination, which he received in March 1723 by Bishop Green of Norwich. He was then licensed as a missionary of the Society for the Propagation of the Gospel in Foreign Parts. Dr. Cutler's move, however, from Congregationalism to Anglicanism won him no friends among emerging American patriots and the non-Anglican religious community. He was subsequently informed that his services would no longer be needed at Yale. In any case, welcomed by non-Puritans, he was assigned as the first rector of Old North Church, where he served from 1723 to 1765, the year he died (December 29).

One can only wonder what it was that motivated this distinguished clergyman of such standing to invite the young Charles Wesley, after only a day and a half of acquaintance, to preach at Old North Church. Was it curiosity about a young priest who had been serving on the "frontier" in Georgia? Was there a winsomeness about the young Wesley? Was Wesley's visit, as a representative of the mother church, an important signal to a community filled with Congregationalists, Presbyterians, Puritans, Dissenters? Was Cutler poorly prepared with his own sermon for Sunday, September 26? One is left to one's imagination. This much is clear, however: Wesley was on his way back to England with official reports from Governor Oglethorpe of Georgia to proper authorities in London, and he would be able to take messages in person to the Bishop of London. Furthermore, it seems highly unlikely that Dr. Cutler would have invited Charles to preach from his pulpit, if there had not been something about Wesley that convinced him that this was a young man with something to say and someone to whom he could entrust the people of his parish and the pulpit of his church.

There must have been a sense of trust and confidence in the young priest, Charles Wesley, on the part of Dr. Cutler, since his son, John, who was to enter the ministry, left with Wesley for passage on the same ship to England for his ordination.

Mr. John Checkley[9]

On his first Sunday in Boston, September 26, Wesley notes in his *MSJ* that, after preaching at Christ Church and at King's Chapel, he spent the evening with Mr. "Chicheley." The name is misspelled by Wesley. This gentleman was unquestionably John Checkley, who was born in the year 1680 in Boston. He owned a shop in the middle of Boston, where he sold books, medicines, and other small articles, and the shop was a popular gathering place. He was

---

9. See the extended discussion about John Checkley in Danker, "Younger Brother Unveiled," 14–18.

an ardent supporter of the Church of England and a noted church Controversalist. This is demonstrated by the fact that he went to England three times for ordination but because of opposition by his enemies, especially Presbyterians, failed to receive it until he was sixty years old (1739). He then served South Providence from 1739 to 1754, the year he died (April 15). This means Checkley was still seeking ordination at the time Charles Wesley was in Boston. In Wesley's record of the first encounter with Checkley on September 26, he described him as "a right honest zealous advocate for the Church of England, who has on that account, been cruelly persecuted by the Presbyterians."[10]

In the colony Checkley had been more than a nominal Controversialist. He was such a staunch loyalist that he had published tracts opposing Presbyterians and others who were not within the fold of the Church of England.[11] On one occasion he was even brought to trial for libelous activity in this regard:

> Mr. Checkley . . . went to England, in 1728, to apply for holy orders, but he had succeeded in rousing against him the enmity of the whole New England Church; and a letter from two of its ministers to Bishop Gibson led that prelate to refuse him ordination, as being an enemy of the House of Hanover, an enemy to all other Christian denominations, and an uneducated man—three charges which were all peculiarly offensive to that eminent scholar and catholic Whig bishop. Checkley returned to Boston to busy himself in the affairs of the church, as is indicated by our later records.[12]

The amount of time Wesley spent with Checkley during the month in Boston is quite significant, for there are four *MSJ* entries that mention him. On October 12, Wesley recorded:

---

10. *MSJ* 1:56.

11. Foote said Checkley was a "representative of the most extreme opinions of the High Church party both in church and state" (Foote, *Annals of King's Chapel*, 1:285).

12. Foote, *Annals of King's Chapel*, 1:304.

> Supped with several of the clergy at Mr. Checkley's, who entertained us very agreeably with his adventures. He seems to have excellent natural parts, much solid learning, and true primitive piety; is acquainted with the power, and therefore holds fast the form of godliness; obstinate as my father, in good, and not to be borne down by evil.[13]

Checkley has probably related to Charles some of the experiences he had endured in having his ordination in the Church of England opposed. It is interesting that two days later, October 14, Wesley made this entry in his *MSJ*:

> Was taken up with the clergy, in drawing up recommendation of him [Checkley] to the Bishop of London for orders. The bishop had been formerly frightened from ordaining him, by the outcries of the Presbyterians. They were wise to keep a man out of the ministry who had in a private capacity approved himself such a champion of the Church.[14]

Again on October 17, Wesley spent time with Mr. Checkley. They discussed "spiritual religion" and the latter's wife observed that much of Wesley's thinking was like that of William Law. Wesley was delighted to hear Law mentioned and discovered that Checkley's wife was well acquainted with William Law's *Serious Call to a Devout and Holy Life* (1729). He learned that she owned one of the two copies of the book in New England, which Wesley immediately borrowed. He spent an evening reading it to the Williams family, with whom he was staying. According to Wesley's account the reading seems to have had a strong influence on Mr. Williams and his daughter.

Ryan Danker suggests in his article, "The Younger Brother Unveiled: Charles Wesley and Anglicanism in Colonial Boston,"[15] that the Williams mentioned in Wesley's *MSJ* is Dr. Nathaniel Williams, "a Puritan minister, a schoolmaster, and a physican in

---

13. *MSJ* 1:57.
14. *MSJ* 1:57.
15. Danker, "Younger Brother Unveiled," 22.

Boston."[16] This is indeed an interesting suggestion, as it expands the young Wesley's contacts beyond the Anglican associates about whom there are specific references in the *MSJ*. The association with a Puritan clergyman would be difficult to understand were it not for the fact that Williams was a physician and while in Boston, Charles suffered from dire health issues, as his *MSJ* makes clear. "If Williams is the man in the journal, he would be one of the only Puritans that Charles mentions apart from a courtesy visit he paid to the governor upon his arrival and the only Puritan with whom he spent any amount of time."[17]

In the only known extant letter written from Boston to his brother John, Charles remarked of Checkley:

> I find he has, throughout his life, been persecuted, only not to death, by the spirit of Presbytery. It has reduced him and his family to the last extremity. He has excellent natural parts, much solid learning, and true primitive piety, is acquainted with the power and therefore holds fast the form of godliness; obstinate as was my father, in good, and like him not to be borne down by evil.[18]

Finally, there is a mention of Mr. Checkley on Monday, October 25. Checkley brings the message that Charles Wesley was to board the ship. When they arrived at the wharf, however, Wesley had to wait in the cold for half an hour.[19] His *MSJ* entry says, "Mr. Checkley helped me into the boat and covered me up." Wesley was quite sick at the time and concerned about exposure to the cold weather.

It seems that through Wesley's encounters with Checkley he was convinced that the latter was a man of honor, capability, and spiritual depth, and worthy of ordination. Perhaps the assistance Charles gave by writing a recommendation for him to the Bishop of

16. Danker, "Younger Brother Unveiled," 22.

17. Danker, "Younger Brother Unveiled," 23. Apparently Thomas Prince's diary indicates an association between Dr. Williams and John Checkley, as noted in Shipton, *Sibley's Harvard Graduates*, 4:185.

18. At the conclusion see the complete three-part letter, which includes entries for October 17, 18, 21, and 25.

19. *MSJ* 1:59.

London exercised some of the influence necessary for the bishop to reverse his previously negative decision and to ordain Checkley. The bishop did change his mind, and Checkley was ordained in 1739.

Mr. Jonathan Belcher

On Monday, September 30, we learn that Wesley visited the governor, Jonathan Belcher, grandson of Andrew Belcher, a tavern-keeper in Cambridge during the early days of Harvard College. Jonathan Belcher's father, Andrew, however, became a wealthy Boston merchant and councilor of the province and sent his son to Harvard where he graduated in 1699. Belcher's selection as governor did not make many loyalists happy, for he was American born. Yet it was precisely this fact that he used as an argument to convince the proper authorities that he was the right choice at the time. He was sympathetic with the Congregationalists and a Dissenter, though he acted as if the King's Chapel in Boston were really his domain. Why did Charles Wesley go to visit him? Perhaps his official relationship as the secretary of the governor of Georgia motivated him to seek out the governor of Massachusetts for conversation.

Here is Dr. Cutler's opinion of the new governor:

> Very mortifying to the Church here is the Governor, whom we expect every day, Jonathan Belcher, Esq. Not long ago this gentleman married his daughter here to a person baptised and brought up in the Church; but not before he had strictly obliged him entirely to forsake the Church, which the booby has faithfully done.[20]

It must be said in Belcher's defense, however, that he succeeded in garnering the support of King George II for Old North Church (Christ Church). Over a three-year period the King sent the following gifts to the church: a silver Holy Communion set, a Bible, prayer books, a damask, cushions, and vestments. The Communion silver is housed in the Boston Museum of Fine Arts.

---

20. Foote, *Annals of King's Chapel*, 1:398.

The Rev. Ebenezer Miller

During the afternoon of September 30, Charles Wesley was visited by Mr. Millar (misspelled in the *MSJ*; should be Miller), "a good-natured clergyman."[21] This was Ebenezer Miller (died 1763), holder of the Doctor of Divinity from Harvard College, and MA and DD degrees from Oxford. Miller was the brother of John Checkley's wife. He was assigned to a mission in South Braintree (later Christ Church, Quincy), where he served from 1727 to 1761. Miller was a native-born New Englander and part of a well-known and respected Braintree family. On October 4 Wesley recorded, "I rode with Mr. and Mrs. Price, Dr. Cutler (his son, and Mr. Brig, two Cambridge scholars), to see Mr. Miller, at Braintree."[22] Clearly it is The Rev. Ebenezer Miller who was serving at Braintree whom Charles Wesley mentioned. Miller was also not immune to criticism:

> Dr. Miller was well versed in the history and doctrines of the Church, and not afraid to meet in public polemic discussion Parson Dunbar of the First Church, who accused him of having been sent by his superiors to 'foment disturbances' and 'cause divisions' among the churches of New England, and by "promoting Episcopacy, to increase the political influence of the Crown."[23]

The last entry in the *MSJ* mentioning Mr. Miller is on October 18:

> Accordingly Mr. Miller came very early to attend me to the ship. I took occasion to mention the book I had borrowed of his sister, Mrs Checkley, and read him the characters of Cognatus and Uranius. He liked them much and promised he would carefully read the whole.[24]

---

21. *MSJ* 1:56.
22. *MSJ* 1:56.
23. Foote, *Annals of King's Chapel*, 1:259.
24. *MSJ* 1:58.

The Rev. Addington Davenport

On October 4, after an outing to Braintree with The Rev. and Mrs. Price and Dr. Cutler, as well as Cutler's son and a Mr. Brig, both students at Cambridge, Charles Wesley learned that a Mr. Davenport had come to visit him. Wesley described him as "a worthy clergyman, as deserving of the name as any I see in New England."[25]

Who was this man who had come to call on Wesley? He was The Rev. Mr. Addington Davenport, who was born on May 16, 1701, and graduated from Harvard College in 1719, and received the MA from Oxford on March 12, 1732. Charles received his BA degree from Oxford in 1730 and his MA degree in 1733. Therefore, he and Davenport had been students during the same time at Oxford. Whether they knew each other then is not known. In 1732 Davenport was appointed by the Society for the Propagation of the Gospel in Foreign Parts and became the second missionary at St. Andrew's Church in Scituate, where he served from 1732 to 1737. Afterwards from 1737 to 1740 he was the assistant at King's Chapel (Boston), and in May of 1740 he became the first rector of Trinity Church in Boston, which was built in 1733.

There is no indication that Charles Wesley had any association with the Trinity Church or its clergy during the time of his visit in Boston. The Rev. Davenport was still serving St. Andrew's Church in Scituate at the time. He did not become rector at Trinity Church until the spring of 1737, as indicated, and by that time Wesley had departed Boston.

Why would Davenport have come to call on Charles Wesley? Had they known of each other at Oxford, or had Davenport heard of Wesley's association with Oxford University and, hence, wanted to meet this man with whom he shared a common background? Perhaps the word had spread rather quickly that Wesley had preached the previous two Sundays at King's Chapel and at Old North Church (Christ Church) and on the latter of those Sundays, October 3, he also assisted with the administration of Holy Communion at Old

---

25. *MSJ* 1:57.

North Church. Unfortunately we do not know if there was a specific reason for Davenport's calling on Wesley.

Mr. Peter Appee

This is someone whom Charles Wesley probably wished he had never met. He was a Dutchman, who had taken passage to the New World on the ship *Simmonds* at the same time Charles made the voyage in 1735. At first he seemed to be quite serious about religion but then turned out to be somewhat of a con artist. Apparently he had intended to marry a certain Miss Bovey, whom he met in Georgia, after he had returned to Holland and had gotten some personal and business matters in order. Miss Bovey, a beautiful young woman mentioned by Charles in the Georgia section of his *MSJ*, however, died quite suddenly, and her death is mentioned in John Wesley's records as well.

Appee had plagued Wesley about religion, as well as money. He even tried to procure loans from him with no intent to repay them. In a letter entry dated October 21, Wesley records: "Appee, like an errant gentleman as he is, has drawn me into monstrous expenses for ship stores, etc."[26] Given his deceitful behavior on numerous occasions, one cannot be convinced that anything he said had one iota of truth. While in Boston, Appee continued to be an annoyance to Wesley. According to the *MSJ*, on October 21, when Wesley was very sick,

> Appee came, and laboured all he could to dissuade me from the voyage [i.e., his return to England], promising himself to deliver my letters and papers, and excuse me to Mr. Oglethorpe. Mr. Price, Williams, etc., joined with him. But I put an end to their importunity by assuring them nothing less than death should hinder my embarking.

. . .

Friday, October 22. It may be of use hereafter to remember Appee's behaviour at Boston. He gave out that his

---

26. See complete letter at the end of this chapter.

design in coming to Georgia had been to take charge of the people there. But finding Mr. Oglethorpe just as genius as himself, he thought his own stay there was not so necessary, but he might safely quit the interest of the colony, which, had it not been to such an hand, he could never have prevailed on himself to do. That at present he was unresolved where to bestow himself; only that it should be on that part of mankind which needed him the most. That he was going to England about matters of the last importance. Two or three letters of no moment, he said, I carried; but all secret dispatches to the Duke of Newcastle, and other ministers of state, he was charged with. From the court of Great Britain he was to be sent envoy to Spain. His money, a few hundreds of pounds, he had (in some companies) sent before him to England; in others had turned it into silver, and freighted Indivine's ship.[27]

Typical of Appee's behavior is what transpired after Charles Wesley finally got on board the ship *Hannah* on October 25, to depart for England. Once on board, having been so ill, he lay down in a state room, noting that he was "less fatigued . . . than I expected."[28] Nevertheless, Appee, who knew how sick Wesley had been, came on board and told Wesley that he wanted the state-room where he was resting, since it was assigned to him.

Dr. Graves (misspelled; should be Greaves)

Thomas Greaves (pronounced "Graves"), who practiced medicine in Boston, was consulted by Charles Wesley during his visit. Greaves was an active member of Christ Church during its early years and a significant contributor toward the costs of building the church. He also served as First Senior Warden, and subsequently was a member of the vestry at various times. He was also an original pew owner. It seems that in 1736 he was serving as a judge for the Superior Court of the Province.

27. *MSJ* 1:58–59.
28. *MSJ* 1:59.

On October 9 Wesley recorded, "Was dragged out to consult Dr. Graves about my increasing flux. He prescribed a vomit, from which I received much benefit."[29] Yet on Monday, October 25, Wesley stated in his *MSJ*, "This morning Dr. Graves came over from Charlestown to see me, gave me physic, and advice."[30] Is this the same Dr. Graves whom Charles consulted on October 9? It is assumed so.

The Plasteds, Mr. and Mrs. Williams, Dr. Gibbons, Dr. Gardner

To date I have been unable to locate any background information on the following persons of whom Charles Wesley also writes in the *MSJ*: The Plasteds, Mr. and Mrs. Williams, Dr. Gibbons and Dr. Gardener.

Wesley notes on October 5 that he dined at Mr. Plasted's, "a London acquaintance of my brother's who from thence took occasion to find me out, and showed me all the friendship and civility he could, while I stayed in Boston."[31]

As peviously noted, Wesley apparently stayed for a number of days in the home of the Williams family while in Boston, which seems unusual given Williams's Puritan associations. Of course, an opportunity to read from William Law's *Serious Call* to Williams and his daughter, which impressed them, was attractive to Charles.

Wesley's sojourn in Boston is marked by happy times, especially his encounters and fellowship with the Anglican clergy of Boston and the surrounding area. He seems to circulate quite freely and with ease among them, such as Dr. Cutler and The Rev. Price, who held distinguished positions in the colony, and among those who were serving mission stations, such as The Rev.

---

29. *MSJ* 1:57.
30. *MSJ* 1:59.
31. *MSJ* 1:57.

Miller. According to Charles Wesley's *MSJ*, some of them apparently sought him out as well, e.g., Davenport and Miller.

Experiences and Places

Priestly Functions:

(a) Preaching—According to Wesley's *MSJ*, he preached six times during his stay in Boston, twice on each of the succeeding Sundays: September 26, October 3, and October 10. On September 26 and October 3, he preached at Old North Church (Christ Church) in the morning and in the afternoon at King's Chapel. He records that he preached twice on October 10, but provides no record of where or when. The sermon he preached on September 26 was entitled "The One Thing Needful."[32] On October 3, he preached on the text "There the wicked cease from troubling, and there the weary are at rest [Job 3:17]." He preached the same sermon in the afternoon to the congregation of King's Chapel. There is no indication of either sermon topics or biblical readings for October 10, and there is no record in the *MSJ* that he preached on Sunday, October 17 or 24. There is no entry for Sunday, October 24.

(b) Sacrament of Holy Communion—According to Wesley's record of Sunday, October 3, he received the Sacrament of Holy Communion for the first time in two months: "After near two months' want of it, I again enjoyed the benefit of the Sacrament, which I assisted Dr. Cutler to administer."[33] This would indicate that on his first Sunday in Boston, September 26, when he preached at Christ Church in the morning and King's Chapel in the afternoon, he did not receive or administer the Sacrament. Perhaps the services on September 26 were Morning Prayer and Evening Prayer.

---

32. *MSJ* 1:55. Charles transcribed a number of his brother John's sermons, of which this is one. See Heitzenrater, "Early Sermons," 150-61; cf. Newport. *Sermons*, 79, 360-68.

33. *MSJ* 1:56.

THE BOSTON SOJOURN

There is one other entry in the *MSJ* for the Boston visit which records participation in the sacrament of Holy Communion. It is on October 10: "Recovered a little strength in the Sacrament."[34] There are no records for the Sundays October 17 and 24, that Wesley either received or administered the Sacrament and no indication that on the weekdays, as was often his practice, that he received or celebrated the Sacrament.

Places Visited by Charles Wesley

Aside from his stay in Boston proper, Wesley visited a number of places in the surrounding area on three successive days—October 2, 4, and 5. (a) On October 2, he made an excursion into the countryside with The Rev. Price:

> I rode out with Mr. Price in his chaise, to see the country, which is wonderfully delightful. The only passage out of town is a neck of land about two hundred yards over; all the rest being encircled with the sea. The temperate air, the clear rivulets, and the beautiful hills and dales, which we everywhere met with, seemed to present the very reverse of Georgia.[35]

(b) The following day, October 4, he rode to Braintree with the Prices, Dr. Cutler, his son, and another student from Cambridge to visit The Rev. Miller. Perhaps Miller had extended Wesley an invitation, when he called on Wesley in Boston. (c) And on October 5, after dining with the Plasteds, who, as noted, were London acquaintances of his brother John, he "drove Mr. Cutler to Cambridge. I had only time to observe the civility of the fellows, the regularity of the buildings, and pleasantness of the situation."[36]

There are no *MSJ* entries for October 6, 7, and 8, and one can only assume that he was becoming ill, since on October 9, he noted, "Was dragged out to consult Dr. Graves about my

---

34. *MSJ* 1:57.
35. *MSJ* 1:56.
36. *MSJ* 1:57.

increasing flux."³⁷ There are no other *MSJ* entries indicating that he made further excursions to other places. This was no doubt due to his weakened and ill state.

Illness

Wesley indicated that he was already not feeling well after preaching on October 10: "my body was extremely weakened by preaching twice."³⁸ The day before he consulted a doctor about "my increasing flux [diarrhea]. He prescribed a vomit, from which I received much benefit."³⁹ A week later, on Saturday, October 16, he wrote: "My illness increasing, notwithstanding all the doctors could do for me, I began seriously to consider my condition; and at my evening hour of retirement found benefit from Pascal's prayer on sickness."⁴⁰ The entry for October 19 and 20 states: "I grew worse and worse, and on Thursday, October 21, was forced to keep my chamber through pain."⁴¹ That day he wrote to his brother John, "If my pains have any intermission, the walking up or down stairs or the speaking three sentences, brings them back again."⁴²

From October 22 to 24, he was still trying to overcome his illness. "Within that time," Wesley says, "I vomited, purged, bled, sweated, and took laudanum, which entirely drained me of the little strength I had left."⁴³ The lack of an entry for October 24, may have been due to illness. The following day, October 25, he felt "surprisingly better, though not yet able to walk."⁴⁴ That same day Dr. Greaves came to visit him, examined him, and wrote out some instructions for medical care. This was the same day Wesley finally

37. *MSJ* 1:57.
38. *MSJ* 1:57.
39. *MSJ* 1:57.
40. *MSJ* 1:57.
41. *MSJ* 1:58.
42. See complete letter at the end of this chapter.
43. *MSJ* 1:58.
44. *MSJ* 1:59.

boarded the ship to depart for England. However, it was a very difficult day for this very ill man. Rev. Price drove him to the wharf, but when they got there the ship was not ready for boarding. Therefore, Charles was forced to wait half an hour in the cold air. When he finally boarded a smaller boat to take him to the ship, it took another two hours just to reach the ship *Hannah* and board.

On October 26, the day the ship finally was clear of all land, Wesley stated in his *MSJ*: "Entered upon the doctor's regimen, and quickly found the benefit."[45]

Correspondence

One cannot conclude a discussion of "Charles Wesley's Boston Sojourn" without giving careful consideration to the letters he wrote while in Boston. Only one *MSJ* entry indicates that he corresponded while in Boston. On October 1 he recorded: "I wrote to my brother concerning my return to Georgia, which I found myself inclined to refer wholly to God."[46] Frank Baker indicates, however, in his study, *Charles Wesley As Revealed by His Letters*, that Charles wrote a number of letters while in Boston.

On October 5 and 6, Charles wrote a lengthy letter to his brother John in an interestingly coded fashion. The brothers had already endured many difficulties with intercepted letters opened by others, and Charles was determined to avoid that difficulty by writing this letter in Latin, Greek, and shorthand. Baker cites the one English longhand passage:

> October 6. If you are as desirous as I am of a correspondence, you must set upon Byrom's shorthand immediately. I leave my journal and other papers with Mr. Price, which he will send you if I fall short of England.[47]

The letter is filled with reflections on the conflicts and despair experienced in Georgia and indicates Charles's uneasiness about

---

45. *MSJ* 1:59.
46. *MSJ* 1:56.
47. Baker, *Charles Wesley as Revealed by His Letters*, 26.

the future. All of the slanderous insults he endured while in Georgia continued to plague him. Nevertheless, he knew his own heart and that he had a clear conscience. Here is a brief passage transcribed from shorthand by Frank Baker:

> Dear Brother,
>
> I take (advantage?) of the deepest seriousness and best temper I have known since the fatal hour I left Oxford, to lay open my very heart, as I call God to witness that what I now write comes from it. You know what has passed in Georgia. . . . The snare is broken, and I am delivered by the only expedient that could have saved me. . . . I sometimes think how to dispose of the remainder of a (mad?) life. I can either live at Oxford or with my brother, who before I left England had provided for me without my asking. He will labour all he can to settle me. But I trust God will not suffer me to set up my rest there.[48]

The letter indicates that Commissary Price had offered Wesley a church in Boston or the surrounding area, but Charles continued in shorthand:

> But Georgia alone can give me the solitude I seek after. I cannot look for a long life there, but neither do I count that a blessing.[49]

After all the turmoil Wesley had endured in Georgia and on board the ship with Captain Indivine, it is not surprising that he needed time alone for reflection. Boston, however, hardly afforded him that privilege. He wrote to John:

> I am wearied with this hospitable people, they so vex and tease me with their civilities. They do not suffer me to be alone. The clergy, who come from the country on a visit, drag me along with them when they return. I am constrained to take a view of this New England, more pleasant even than the old. I cannot help exclaiming,

---

48. Baker, *Charles Wesley as Revealed by His Letters*, 27.
49. Baker, *Charles Wesley as Revealed by His Letters*, 27.

"O happy country, that cherishes neither *flies*, nor *crocodiles*, nor *informers*."[50]

Not only was Charles experiencing inner unrest over excess hospitality and civility; he was greatly disturbed physically and emotionally because of the illness that had begun in Georgia and which he thought he had shaken. No doubt the following passage was written to John before he consulted Dr. Greaves:

> My disorder, once removed by this most salubrious air, has again returned. All my friends advise me to consult a physician, but I cannot afford so expensive a funeral.[51]

Three additional excerpts cited by Baker from Charles's letters to John from Boston indicate the kind of mood swings the young priest was experiencing as he contemplated departing for England:

> **October 15:**
>
> I should be glad for your sake to give a satisfactory account of myself, but that you must never expect from me. It is fine talking while we have youth and health on our side; but sickness would spoil your boasting as well as mine. . . .
>
> Though I am apt to think that I shall at length arrive in England to deliver what I am entrusted with, yet do I not expect, or wish for, a long life. How strong must the principle of self-preservation be, which can make such a wretch as I am willing to live at all!—Or rather unwilling to die; for I know no greater pleasure in life, than in considering that it cannot last for ever. . . . I am just now much worse than ever; but nothing less than death shall hinder me from embarking.

The most revealing letter is one bearing entries on four specific dates: October 17, 18, 21, and 25. The entire text of the letter is included here:

---

50. Baker, *Charles Wesley as Revealed by His Letters*, 27.
51. Baker, *Charles Wesley as Revealed by His Letters*, 27. See also Whitehead, *John Wesley*, 1:141–42.

Friday, Boston

Dear Brother,

If I ever see England, it will be by that time this reaches you. My poor friend here has not yet convinced me of your hypocrisy but I take for granted you have still a disinterested concern for my happiness. I should be glad for your sake, to give a satisfactory account of myself, but that you must never expect from me. They have dragged me at last to a physician, whose prescriptions I have followed hitherto without effect: but he cannot answer for their success unless I could stay a few days on shore, which is impracticable. 'Tis fine talking while we have youth and health on our side; but sickness would spoil your marooning, as well as mine. I am now glad of a warm bed, but must quickly betake myself to my board again, וגם זה לטוב [Hebrew: moreover, this would be for good].

Though I am apt to believe I shall at length arrive in England and to deliver what I am entrusted with, yet do I not expect or wish for a long life. How strong must the principle of self-preservation be, which can make such a wretch as me willing to live at all!—Or rather unwilling to die; for I know no greater pleasure in life, than in considering [that] it cannot last for ever! . . .

The temptations past[52]
No none shall vex me; every grief I feel
Shortens the destined number, every pulse
Beats a sharp moment of the pain away,
And the last stroke will come. By swift degrees
Time sweeps me off, and I shall soon arrive
At life's sweet period. O Celestial Point
That ends this mortal story!

---

52. See Watts, *Horae Lyricae*, Book II, "Sacred Vertue, Loyalty, and Friendship." Wesley reverses the first line "The temptations past" which reads "The past Temptations" in the original. In line 2, he changes "vex us" to "vex me" and in line 6, "we shall" to "I shall." He apparently omitted line 4, "Beats a sharp moment of the pain away."

THE BOSTON SOJOURN

Today completes my three weeks unnecessary stay in Boston. Tomorrow the ship falls down. I am just now much worse than ever, but nothing less than death shall hinder my embarking. Mr. Oglethorpe I know will gladly excuse my writing. I should write to my two other Georgia friends, would pain permit. Don't forget poor Lasserre.

October 18. A blast attends all that belongs to me. The ship that carries me must move with endless delays. 'Tis well if it sails this week. I have lived so long in honours and indulgences that I have almost forgot whereunto I am called; being strongly urged to set up rest here. But I will lean no longer upon men. When I again put myself in the power of any of my own merciless species, either expecting their kindness or desiring their esteem. Ἀνελθέτο Φρεδερείκη! [Let him go to Frederica! (i.e., Let him go to Hades!)]

I must mention an unhappy matter to you. Mr. John Checkley, and *valeat quantum valere potest* [let him be strong in so far as he is able]. By the strictest enquiry of friends and enemies, I find he has been throughout his life, persecuted, only not to death, by the spirit of Presbytery. It has reduced him and his family to the last extremity. He has excellent natural parts, much solid learning, and true primitive piety, is acquainted with the power and therefore holds fast the form of godliness; obstinate as was my father in good, and not to be borne down by evil. Κάλος Στρατιώτης [a good soldier]; "Αοκνος Θεοδρόμος [God's untiring runner]; "Ακμων τυπόμεος [an anvil when it is beaten]. Mr. Oglethorpe himself does not better understand nor is more beloved by the Indians than he: he is activity itself. Made for abstinence and hardships. But for his family he had taken a walk over now to see Mr. Oglethorpe. He has studied America, as much as most men in it. I carry recommendations of him to the Bishop of London, who was formerly frightened by his pretended Jacobitism from admitting him into Holy Orders, to which he has for about these twenty years devoted himself.

He understands surveying and fortification: on which and one thousand other accounts I thought he might be of great use in Georgia, but could not venture proposing it [to] him without first obtaining Mr. Oglethorpe's directions. Should I die in the passage, you are at liberty to give him anything that was mine. My sole heir and executor at Tiverton, I am sure, will consent to it. Appee, like an errant gentleman as he is, has drawn me into monstrous expenses for ship stores, etc., so that what with my three-week's stay at Charlestown, my month's stay here, and my double passage, from Courtier I am turned philosopher. But this I absolutely forbid your mentioning to Mr. [Oglethorpe], except in the above case of my death. Then add to the account of my life "laid down in his service," and let him judge on whose side is the balance. **October 21.** I am worried on all sides by my friends' solicitations to defer my winter's voyage till I have recovered a little strength. So far I agree with you and the physicians that to go in my condition is running upon certain death. If my pains have any intermission, the walking up or down stairs, or the speaking three sentences, brings them back again. Mr. [_____], I am apt to think, would allow me to wait a fortnight for the next ship; but then, if I recover, my stay will be thought unnecessary. I must die to prove myself sick, and I can do no more at sea. I am therefore determined to be carried on board tomorrow morning and leave the event to God. **October 25.** The ship fell down as was expected, but providence sent a contrary wind that hindered my following till now. Since the 21st, I have tried the virtue of vomits, purges, bleeding, and opiates. I am at present something better. On board the *Hannah,* Captain Corney [i.e., Cornish?]; in the state-room, which they have forced upon me. I have not strength for more. Adieu![53]

---

53. A copy of this letter is found in the Frank Baker Collection of the Divinity School of Duke University. I am grateful to Dr. Richard P. Heitzenrater for making it available to me.

Summary and Evaluation

What are we to make of this unexpected visit of Charles Wesley to Boston? Clearly, though a young priest who had just served four months in the colony of Georgia and was on his way back to London, he seemed to attract considerable attention. His immediate invitations to preach at the most prestigious Anglican churches, Old North Church (Christ Church), and King's Chapel, indicate that his presence was regarded as significant. The Boston community was wrought with religious strife and steadily American patriotism was surfacing with increasing tension between people of the Anglican persuasion on the one hand and Puritans, Presbyterians, Congregationalists, and diverse Dissenters on the other. Into this atmosphere of religious tension came a young priest of the Church of England, who must have been a symbol of hope and affirmation to the Boston Anglicans. He was dined, entertained, and placed before the community in the most conspicuous places, namely, the most significant Church of England pulpits of Boston. Wesley seems to have enjoyed himself in Boston, aside from his illness and the overbearing hospitality. He seems to have been comfortable circulating among the Anglican clergy of the colony, and there is no indication that he had previous contact with any clergy of the churches who were increasingly at odds with the Church of England. No doubt he used his position as Governor Oglethorpe's secretary and Secretary for Indian Affairs in Georgia as an entrée to the governor of Massachusetts, Jonathan Belcher, whom he visited shortly after his arrival. There is no record of his conversation with the governor, only a record of the visit itself. Nevertheless, as a man with credentials from the Church of England and Oglethorpe's emissary to the proper authorities in London, when Wesley arrived in Boston, he was received with graciousness and respect.

One thing is very clear, however, from his letters to his brother John at this time. He was in no wise persuaded that he should remain in Boston either to receive an appointment to a church by Commissary Price or long enough to recover from his illness and regain strength before setting out on a voyage home. He was determined to leave at all costs.

What possible impact could the Boston visit have had on Wesley the hymn writer and poet? He was not yet known as a sacred poet, and it was not until after his conversion on May 21, 1738, that he appeared on the sacred literary horizon, destined for enduring notoriety as Britain's greatest eighteenth-century religious poet. His lifelong commitment to ministry within the Anglican Communion is affirmed in his experience with the Anglican clergy and their parishes, which is almost the exclusive sphere of his experience while in Boston. While in his later life he, with his brother John, was an initiator and integral part of the Methodist movement, he never thought of it outside of the Church of England. And the high ecclesiology he espoused in his hymns, which he seems to have begun writing with regularity after his conversion on May 21, 1738, in no sense had been watered down on the American frontier. Certainly the Presbyterians, Puritans, and Congregationalists of Boston had no effect upon him.

By the time George Whitefield came to Boston in September of 1740, however, the attitude toward the Wesleys, Whitefield, and the evangelical movement they were leading within the Church of England had changed radically. On May 9 of that year The Rev. Roger Price of Boston wrote to the Bishop of London: "My Lord, Mr. Whitefield, who is occasion of much debate and enquiry, is expected here the next fall. I shall be glad to receive your Lordship's direction for my behaviour towards him."[54]

Whitefield arrived in Boston on September 18, 1740. The following day he visited King's Chapel and went home with The Rev. Price and visited with Church of England clergy. He was not, however, invited to preach, as was Charles Wesley, at King's Chapel or at Old North Church. He was invited to preach at Old South Meeting House, a popular meeting place for Dissenters, and throngs of people came to hear him. He also preached at the Boston Commons in the open air to thousands of people.

---

54. Foote, *Annals of King's Chapel*, 1:504.

THE BOSTON SOJOURN

On June 15, 1741, not quite a year after Whitefield's first visit to Boston, Mr. Brockwell, who would soon be an assistant at King's Chapel, wrote to the Secretary of the Bishop of London as follows:

> The Wesleys and Whitefield are expected here in the fall. We universally dread the consequences of their coming, and I am sure as to myself I shall be glad of the Society's direction how to behave in such perilous times. The two former, if enemies, are powerful ones—men of great capacities, and fortified by a large fund of learning, whereof Whitefield is destitute, and therefore the victory over him is neither difficult nor glorious, however he may boast in his libelous and scandalous Journals. If the venerable Society please to favour us with their instructions how we are to treat these itinerant Preachers, the sooner the better, that we may be armed against the approach of (I fear) these enemies to our church and constitution.[55]

In 1743 Dr. Cutler summed up Whitefield's first visit to Boston in this way:

> When Mr. Whitefield first arrived here, the whole town was alarmed. He made his first visit to our church on a Friday, and conversed with many of our clergy together and belied them—me especially—when he had done. Being not invited into our pulpits, the Dissenters were highly pleased and engrossed him; and immediately the wellspring, and all hands went to Lecture; and this show kept on all the while he was here. The town was ever alarmed; the streets filled with people, with coaches, with chaises,—all for the benefit of that holy man. The conventicles were crowded; but he chose rather our Common, where multitudes might see him in his awful postures; besides that in one crowded conventicle, before he came in, six were killed with fright. The fellow treated the most venerable with an air of superiority. But he forever lashed and anathematized the Church of England, and that was enough.[56]

---

55. Foote, *Annals of King's Chapel*, 1:509.
56. Foote, *Annals of King's Chapel*, 1:507.

If one turns to the significant amount of secular poetry written by Charles Wesley, which was not published until 1988 and 1992, in volumes one and three of *The Unpublished Poetry of Charles Wesley,* edited by this author and a British colleague, the late Oliver A. Beckerlegge, one gains tremendous insight into the kinds of political views which must have been buttressed by Wesley's visit to Boston, though one cannot say unequivocally that they were shaped by the Boston sojourn.

Charles Wesley was a Tory at heart and a loyal supporter of the crown, and he believed that the throne and magistrates were divinely appointed. He clearly believed in the right of kings to govern personally. The idea of a constitutional monarchy was completely foreign to him, as well as the idea of democracy. Charles also had difficulty separating loyalty to the king and his nation from the essentials of religion. Indeed, they were intimately linked. Here are his lines entitled "For the Magistrates":

> Thou, Lord of lords, and King of kings,
>   The eternal Potentate we own;
> From Thee its Source dominion springs,
>   A stream that issues from Thy throne:
> Thou hast ordained the powers that be,
> Who govern by a grant from Thee.
>
> To George in majesty supreme
>   We bow, as sitting on Thy seat,
> To every ruler sent by him,
>   To every magistrate submit,
> Whose delegated power is Thine,
> Whose whole authority, Divine.[57]

Charles Wesley left unpublished at his death a more than six hundred-line epic poem on the American Revolution and a very large manuscript entitled simply "MS Patriotism." Both are filled with his lyrical admonitions of loyalty to the crown and opposition to the American Revolution and patriotism. He is convinced that the brothers Admiral Viscount Howe and General Howe,

---

57. *PW* 8:278–79, stanzas 1 and 3 of a six-stanza poem.

Commander-in-Chief of the British military during the American War of Independence, are responsible for Britain's loss of the war, and he has no friendly words for them. In the next, concluding chapter of this volume, this matter is carefully examined.

One cannot maintain that Wesley's ideas about the American Revolution and the colonies were directly shaped by his Boston sojourn. However, the persons with whom he associated, perhaps with the exception of Governor Belcher and Dr. Williams, would have in principle supported his views. It is important to point out, nevertheless, that there were some loyal Episcopalians who felt that they could remain loyal to the crown and establish an independently governed Episcopal Church in America. In spite of Wesley's strong views of loyalty to God, crown, and nation, clearly his love extended to all humankind, as indicated in the following hymn from *Hymns for the National Fast, February 8, 1782*:

> When plagues the land o'erflow,
> We share the common woe;
> But our patriotic love
> Is not selfish, nor confined,
> But our yearning bowels move
> Toward the whole afflicted kind.
>
> With every sufferer
> We drop the generous tear
> (Whom Thy tendering Spirit leads,)
> Pity no distinction knows,
> Love for all the wounded bleeds,
> Love embraces friends and foes.[58]

Charles Wesley's time in the colonies was formative for him. He learned much about himself. He became an ardent opponent of slavery for the rest of his life, and he became aware of the need for a spiritual awakening in the New World. The Boston visit was unexpected and placed him once again in the midst of a somewhat "established" Church of England, which he welcomed. He also found himself among a group of clergy serving in Boston

---

58. *PW* 8:323–24.

who had been students and held degrees from Oxford University, which he had attended. One of them, Davenport, overlapped with his tenure at Oxford.

Wesley could not possibly have become aware of all the dynamics of religious discord in the Massachusetts colony during his brief stay.[59] He seems to have been well protected from that by the Anglican clergy. It is quite likely that his views of what was transpiring in the colony were shaped very strongly by the sympathizers to the King and to the Church of England with whom he associated. Unquestionably his opposition to war and discord was buttressed by his American sojourn, and his vision of a people of the earth unified in Christ amid human discord of all types was accentuated and enlivened by the Boston visit.

In spite of the fact that the Boston visit seems to have begun pleasantly and was a welcome contrast to Georgia, on October 17 Charles noted in the letter to his brother John cited above,

> Today completes my three weeks' unnecessary stay in Boston. . . . 'Tis well if it sails this week. I have lived so long in honours and indulgences that I have almost forgot whereunto I am called; being strongly urged to set up rest here. But I will lean no longer upon men. When I again put myself in the power of any of my own merciless species, either expecting their kindness or desiring their esteem. . . .
>
> Tomorrow the ship falls down. I am just now much worse than ever, but nothing less than death shall hinder my embarking.

Charles Wesley was delighted finally to depart for England.

---

59. For a detailed discussion of the political and religious context of Boston before, during, and after Wesley's visit, see Danker, "Younger Brother Unveiled."

Chapter 3

Charles Wesley and Slavery[1]

AS PREVIOUSLY NOTED, ONE of the primary transforming forces in Charles Wesley's life was the formation of a lifelong opposition to slavery. While there was no slavery in Georgia at the time of his sojourn there, it was before his departure from Charleston that one learns of his encounter with the horrors of slavery, as recorded in his journal.[2] What other information in the life of Charles is relevant to his posture on slavery?

When Charles Wesley was born in the year 1707 in Epworth, some British traders were actively engaged in the African slave trade. To what extent he may have been influenced by the knowledge of this reality during his childhood and youth we do not know. There does not appear to be evidence that his upbringing by parents Samuel and Susanna would have prejudiced him against persons of other races. Apparently his first encounter with the horrors of slavery was after his departure from the colony of Georgia, when he made his way overland to the port city of Charleston to depart for England.

---

1. This chapter was published previously under this title in *PCWS* 13 (2009) 35–51. It is published here with some additions and revisions.

2. *MSJ* 1:46–47.

Encounter with Slavery in Charleston

The entry in his *MSJ* for Monday, August 2, 1736, reads as follows:

> I had observed much, and heard more, of the cruelty of masters towards their negroes; but now I received an authentic account of some horrid instances thereof. The giving a child a slave of its own age to tyrannize over, to beat and abuse out of sport, was, I myself saw, a common practice. Nor is it strange, that being thus trained up in cruelty, they should afterwards arrive at so great perfection in it: that Mr. Star, a gentleman I often met at Mr. Lasserre's, should, as he himself informed Lasserre, first nail up a negro by the ears, then order him to be whipped in the severest manner, and then to have scalding water thrown all over him, so that the poor creature could not stir for four months after. Another much applauded punishment is drawing their slaves' teeth. One Colonel Lynch is universally known to have cut off a poor negro's legs; and to kill several of them every year by his barbarities.
>
> It were endless to recount all the shocking instances of diabolical cruelty which these men (as they call themselves) daily practice upon their fellow-creatures; and that on the most trivial occasions. I shall only mention one more, related to me by a Swiss gentleman, Mr. Zouberbuhler, an eyewitness of Mr. Hill, a dancing-master in Charlestown. He whipped a she-slave so long, that she fell down at his feet for dead. When by the help of a physician, she was so far recovered, as to show signs of life, he repeated the whipping with equal rigour, and concluded with dropping hot sealing wax upon her flesh. Her crime was overfilling a tea-cup.
>
> These horrid cruelties are the less to be wondered at, because the government itself in effect countenances and allows them to kill their slaves by the ridiculous penalty appointed for it, of about 7 pounds sterling (half of which is usually saved by the criminal's informing against himself). This I can look upon as no other than a public act to indemnify murder.[3]

3. *MSJ* 1:46–47.

We do not know exactly what Charles means by the words "I had observed much, and heard more, of the cruelty of masters towards their negroes." Had he "observed much, and heard more" while on board the ship *Simmonds* on his way to America, while in Georgia, or is he referring to earlier knowledge while in England? Unfortunately, we do not know. What we do know for certain is that at twenty-nine years of age in Charleston he became an eyewitness to the terrifying inhumanity of slavery. He was apparently actively engaged in conversation with Mr. Laserre and Mr. Zouberbuhler about slavery, for he relates information the two men shared with him about three slave owners: Mr. Star, Colonel Lynch, and Mr. Hill, all of whom disclose instances in which they have tortured their slaves in hideous ways. Of these three persons, apparently Charles had met only Mr. Star, though it seems that the information about Star's abuse of slaves came from Mr. Laserre, rather than directly from Mr. Star himself to Wesley.

Charles seems overwhelmed by "these horrid cruelties" toward African slaves and all the more by the reality that the British government sanctioned the killing of slaves by their masters for the payment of a minuscule penalty of seven pounds sterling. In his judgment, this was "a public act to indemnify murder."

The above passage in Wesley's *MSJ* is crucial to the subject of this study for the two realities it establishes: (1) Charles had a firsthand encounter with slavery in an American colony, and (2) he concluded that the government he would support throughout his life was absolutely wrong to allow the murder of slaves by their owners.

In 1735, the year before Charles Wesley arrived in America, the House of Commons passed legislation banning slavery within the colony of Georgia, though it was already entrenched in the area north of Georgia that would eventually become known as South Carolina. Interestingly Georgia was the only one of the British colonies where slavery was prohibited. The Trustees who founded the colony promoted the ban based on pragmatic political and economic reasons, rather than strong moral grounds. The Spanish presence in nearby Florida was a threat to the security of the

83

colony, and Spain was offering freedom to slaves who would serve in its military. For this reason, any slaves brought into Georgia would most certainly be tempted to aid the Spanish, thus threatening the relatively weak English colony.

The Georgia Trustees also genuinely believed that it would be better to avoid another plantation economy and to establish a settlement where persons worked for themselves. They envisaged an economy free of slave labor. While it is not the purpose of this study to discuss the eventual emergence of slavery in Georgia, it should be noted that on May 19, 1749, the Trustees of the colony petitioned the king to repeal the Act of 1735 that prohibited slavery. The petition was approved on October 26, 1749, and slavery became legal in Georgia as of January 1, 1751. Two of the staunchest advocates of this action were James Habersham and George Whitefield, who himself became a slave owner.

The point of this brief historical review is to emphasize that during Charles Wesley's five-month stay in Georgia he had no direct contact with slaves or the institution of slavery. This is not to suggest that he heard nothing about slavery while there. What we may assume from the record of his *MSJ* is that his initial encounter with slavery took place upon his arrival in Charleston.

Other Documents Involving Charles Wesley and Slavery

In addition to Charles Wesley's journal entry of August 2, 1736, there are a few other documents of primary interest that are related to the subject of slavery that shall be addressed here: (1) his *MSJ* record of direct contact with and ministry to "a poor black that had robbed his master" (July 12, 15, 17, 18, 1738); (2) a few poetical references to American slavery; (3) depositions in the Court of King's Bench[4] of William Floyd, a mariner from the City of Bristol, and Little Ephraim Robin John and Ancona Robin Robin John of Old Town, Old Calabar, on the coast of Africa, who were captured and

---

4. See the extracts of the depositions in *AM* (1783) 98–99, 151–53, 211–12.

enslaved but were eventually freed during a sojourn in England and became acquainted with Charles Wesley while staying in Bristol; (4) Charles Wesley's personal letters to William Perronet (January 23, 1774) and Vincent Perronet (November 1, 1775); (5) a series of letters from the above-mentioned former slaves, Ephraim Robin John and Ancona Robin Robin John, to Charles Wesley.

While much concentration in the study of slavery is placed on the colonies of the British Commonwealth, it was also practiced in England proper.[5] In eighteenth-century England to have servants at your command to do the simplest of things, as well as hard labor, was thought by many to be a sign of good breeding, aristocracy, and wealth. While some masters may have treated their slaves equitably, many were horribly abused. At the time of Charles Wesley's return to England, the trade of British slave ships was thriving.

(1) *MSJ of July 1738*. In this passage Charles provides an account of his ministry to a slave who had been imprisoned for stealing from his master. It is a moving encounter.

> **Wednesday, July 12.** Preached at Newgate to the condemned felons. Visited one of them in his cell, sick of a fever—a poor black that had robbed his master. I told him of One who came down from heaven to save lost sinners, and him in particular. Described the sufferings of the Son of God, his sorrows, agony, and death. He listened with all the signs of eager astonishment. The tears trickled down his cheeks while he cried, "What! Was it for me? Did God suffer all this for so poor a creature as me!" I left him waiting for the salvation of God.[6]
>
> . . .
>
> **Saturday, July 15.** Preached there again with an enlarged heart and rejoiced with my poor happy black, who now *believes* the Son of God loved him, and gave himself for him.[7]

---

5. See Gerzina, *Black England*; Fryer, *Staying Power*.
6. *MSJ* 1:136.
7. *MSJ* 1:137.

...

Monday, July 17. Rose free from pain. At Newgate preached on death (which they must suffer the day after tomorrow). Mr. Sparks assisted in giving the Sacrament. Another clergyman was there. Newington asked me to go in the coach with him. At one with the black in his cell, James Hutton assisting. Two more of the malefactors came. I had great help and power in prayer. One rose, and said he felt his heart all on fire, so as he never found himself before; was all in a sweat; believed Christ died for him. I found myself overwhelmed with the love of Christ to sinners. The black was quite happy. The other criminal was in an excellent temper; believing, or on the point of it.[8]

...

Tuesday, July 18. The Ordinary read prayers and preached. I administered the Sacrament to the black, and eight more, having first instructed them in the nature of it. Spake comfortably to them afterwards.

In the cells, one told me that whenever he offered to pray, or had a serious thought, some thing came and hindered him; was with him almost continually; and once appeared. After we had prayed for him in *faith,* he rose amazingly comforted, full of joy and love, so that we could not doubt his having received the atonement.

At night I was locked in with Bray in one of the cells. We wrestled in mighty prayer. All the criminals were present, and all delightfully cheerful. The soldier, in particular, found his comfort and joy increase every moment. Another, from the time he communicated, has been in perfect peace. Joy was visible in all their faces. We sang:

> Behold the Saviour of mankind,
>   Nail'd to the shameful Tree!
> How vast the Love that Him inclined
>   To bleed and die for Thee! etc.[9]

8. *MSJ* 1:137.
9. "On the Crucifixion," stz. 1 (*CPH* 46). This poem is by Samuel Wesley

It was one of the most triumphant hours I have ever known.

Yet on

Wednesday, July 19, I rose very heavy and backward to visit them for the last time. At six prayed and sang with them all together. The Ordinary would read prayers, and preach most miserably. Mr. Sparks and Mr. Broughton present, I felt my heart full of tender love to the latter. He administered. All the ten received. Then he prayed and I after him.

At half-hour past nine their irons were knocked off, and their hands tied. I went in a coach with Sparks, Washington, and a friend of Newington's (Newington himself not being permitted). By half hour past ten we came to Tyburn.[10] Waited till eleven, then were brought the children appointed to die. I got upon the cart with Sparks and Broughton. The Ordinary endeavoured to follow, when the poor prisoners begged he might not come, and the mob kept him down.

I prayed first, then Sparks and Broughton. We had prayed before that our Lord would show there was a power superior to the fear of death. Newington had quite forgot his pain. They were all cheerful; full of comfort, peace, and triumph; assuredly persuaded Christ had died for them and waited to receive them into paradise. Greenaway was impatient to be with Christ.

The black had spied me coming out of the coach, and saluted me with his looks. As often as his eyes met mine, he smiled with the most composed, delightful countenance I ever saw. Read caught hold of my hand in a transport of joy. Newington seemed perfectly pleased. Hudson declared he was never better, or more at ease, in mind and body. None showed any natural terror of death—no fear, or crying, or tears. All expressed their desire of our following them to paradise. I never saw

---

Sr. was salvaged after the fire at the Epworth rectory in February 1709 and was first published in this *Collection*.

10. Tyburn, Middlesex, was the site for hangings in London, near present-day Tyburn Convent on the northern edge of Hyde Park.

such calm triumph, such incredible indifference to dying. We sang several hymns, particularly,

> Behold the Saviour of mankind,
> Nail'd to the shameful Tree . . .

And the hymn entitled "Faith in Christ," which concludes,

> A guilty, weak, and helpless worm,
> Into thy hands I fall.
> Be thou my Life, my Righteousness,
> My Jesus, and my all.[11]

We prayed Him, in earnest faith, to receive their spirits. I could do nothing but rejoice. Kissed Newington and Hudson. Took leave of each in particular. Mr. Broughton bade them not be surprised when the cart should draw away. They cheerfully replied they should not, expressed some concern how we should get back to the coach. We left them going to meet their Lord, ready for the Bridegroom. When the cart drew off, not one stirred, or struggled for life, but meekly gave up their spirits. Exactly at twelve they were turned off. I spoke a few suitable words to the crowd, and returned, full of peace and confidence in our friends' happiness.

That hour under the gallows was the most blessed hour of my life.

Charles Wesley's encounter with this slave condemned to death for his crime of robbery is extremely important in understanding his posture toward the institution of slavery. One must not forget that his 1736 *MSJ* entry in Charleston included the indictment that a specific British law indemnified the murder of slaves. Now he was back in England, and a different British law had condemned a slave to death for robbing his master. In contrast to the rage of the Charleston entry, Wesley here is not overtly concerned with misdirected British law, rather with ministering to a black man who with a group of non-blacks has been sentenced to

---

11. Isaac Watts, "Faith in Christ," stz. 6, included by John Wesley in *CPH* 52. The original is found in Watts, *Hymns and Spiritual Songs* 2.90.

death. According to his *MSJ*, Wesley devotes eight days of pastoral ministry to the prisoners, testifies to their professions of faith and their calmness in the face of death, and accompanies them to their execution. Here we get a glimpse of an evangelical Anglican pastor-priest deeply concerned about the lives, the souls, of these men. Here we see a practitioner of God's grace poured out for all humankind, a hallmark of the Wesleyan movement. There is no privileged class in God's realm. All are the recipients of God's loving grace in Jesus Christ. Wesley shares with the black the central meaning of the gospel and what God has done for him and all others in Jesus Christ and that the salvation offered is for him. The black man is moved to tears.

The formulation of one sentence in the *MSJ* entry of July 17 is of vital importance to this discussion. Wesley writes, "At one with the black in his cell."[12] To the defenders of the institution of slavery it would have been blatant blasphemy to claim that a white and a black could experience oneness. What can Charles possibly mean with the words "one with the black"? Most likely he means unity in Christ, but more. While he never articulated a Christian anthropology as such, here is its basis. There is a common humanity that issues from a Creator whose caring concern for all human beings has been expressed in a self-emptying love that itself is the paradigm for the unity of humankind.

From an ecclesiological perspective, there is more to be mentioned in Charles's account. On July 18 he records: "The Ordinary read prayers and preached. I administered the Sacrament to the black, and eight more, having first instructed them in the nature of it. Spake comfortably to them afterwards."[13] Here Charles functions in his priestly role and shares the elements of Holy Communion with the black and others. How extraordinary is this? There is no mention of baptism, no mention of reception into communicant status of the Church of England. Wesley does say that he instructs the prisoners in the "nature" of the sacrament. This would indicate that they probably had little or no understanding of it.

12. *MSJ* 1:137.
13. *MSJ* 1:138.

This picture of an Anglican priest administering the sacrament to a black man and other condemned prisoners in an English prison is a revealing portrait of the spirit of the Methodist movement, which in 1738 was in its nascence.

(2) *Poetical References to Slavery.* There are only a few references in Charles Wesley's poetry to American slavery. His poem "For the Heathen" was published in *Hymns of Intercession for All Mankind* (1758).[14] From the outset of the Wesleyan movement John and Charles fostered the practice of intercessory prayer among the adherents. Friday noon was a common time appointed for such prayer. It is not surprising that in this collection the formulation of prayers for affairs of the nation (peace and war, e.g., involvement in the Seven Years' War [1756-1763]) and for general concerns of all humankind (childbirth, education, God's sustenance of daily life), would find their way to the printed page from Charles's pen. Such was the collection *Hymns of Intercession for All Mankind*. One poem of this collection is of particular interest to the subject of this chapter. It is titled "For the Heathen."

> 1. Lord over all, if thou hast made,
>   Hast ransom'd every soul of man,
> Why is the grace so long delay'd,
>   Why unfulfil'd the saving plan,
> The bliss for Adam's race design'd
> When will it reach to all mankind?
>
> 2. Art Thou the God of Jews alone,
>   And not the God of Gentiles too?
> To Gentiles make thy goodness known,
>   Thy judgment to the nations shew,
> Awake them by the gospel-call,
> Light of the world, illumine all.
>
> 3. The servile progeny of Ham
>   Seize as the purchase of thy blood,
> Let all the heathen know thy name;
> From idols to the living God,

---

14. *HI* 27-28.

> The dark Americans convert,
> And shine in every pagan heart.
>
> 4. As lightning lanc'd from east to west,
>   The coming of thy kingdom be,
>   To Thee by angel-hosts confest,
>   Bow every soul[15] and every knee,
>   Thy glory let all flesh behold,
>   And then fill up thy heavenly fold.[16]

This poem is the third in a series of prayers for specific religious and ethnic groups: Hymn 32, "For the Jews"; Hymn 33, "For the Turks"; Hymn 34, "For the Heathen"; and Hymn 35, "For the Arians, Socinians, Deists, and Pelagians, etc." "For the Heathen" is the only one of the *Hymns of Intercession* with lines dedicated specifically to African slaves. In stanza 3 he speaks of the "servile progeny of Ham" and refers to them as "dark Americans." His prayer is that they shall be converted. Interestingly it is this stanza that was chosen by his brother John Wesley to conclude his treatise, *Thoughts Upon Slavery* (1774). The last two lines of the poem are extremely important:

> Thy glory let all flesh behold,
> And then fill up thy heavenly fold.

Who is to be included in God's heavenly fold? "All flesh," says Charles. Unquestionably this means the inclusion of all African Americans, all slaves. No one is excluded from the presence of God.

In stanza 3 of Part II[17] of Hymn 10 of a poem titled "To the American Rebels" Charles Wesley once again used the phrase "The servile progeny of Ham." In the poem, he is longing for the day when Jesus shall make wars cease and bring everlasting peace to all humankind.

> The savage Tribes, an unjust Race,

---

15. The original is "sort" but was changed to "soul" in the 1759 edition and following.
16. *HI* 28.
17. *MSP* 23–24; *UP* 1:74.

> Americans shall then embrace
> Their God so long unknown;
> The servile progeny of Ham
> Shall prostrated at Jesus' name
> Their dear Redeemer own.

In the concluding stanzas 4 and 5 of the poem he carries forth the theme of the series of poems in *Hymns of Intercession* by longing for the day when Muslims and Jews will recognize Jesus as the true Messiah and celestial love shall reign over a "new-made earth."

> The Crescent to the Cross shall yield,
> The Turks and Heathen be compel'd
> Their Sovereign to confess,
> And Jews, who pierc'd his hands and side,
> Discern Jehovah crucified,
> Their true Messiah bless.
>
> Then all religious Babels cease,
> And all into the kingdom press
> Of God reveal'd below.
> And fountains open'd from above
> In streams of pure celestial love
> The new-made earth o'erflow.

Charles's message here regarding the enslaved Africans in America is essentially the same as in his poem "For the Heathen," namely, a plea for their conversion. However, it is not mere conversion for conversion's sake, rather that the earth will be made new through overflowing streams of "pure celestial love." In this new world Americans will embrace the "savage tribes," namely, Native Americans. While Charles's own modes of expressing his hopes for Native Americans, African Americans, Muslims, and Jews may be very inadequate, one thing is clear, he longs for a world in which all human beings live in harmony. He holds in tension what is very difficult to maintain—an exclusive faith and an inclusive love.

CHARLES WESLEY AND SLAVERY

Why did Charles, who penned so many poems on national affairs, never address the subject of slavery in poetry, as he had done in the prose of his *MSJ* in 1736? Did he feel that his brother's treatise, *Thoughts Upon Slavery* (1774), was sufficient? Was his concern only an evangelical one, i.e., the conversion of slaves, and not with the evils of the institution? Was he aware of the anti-slavery poems of William Cowper (1731–1800), who was asked by John Newton after his conversion to the anti-slavery movement to write ballads that could be set to music and sung in the streets of England's cities and towns? Cowper's poem, "The Negro's Complaint," reflects the horrors of the Middle Passage, of which he no doubt had heard from Newton.

> Forc'd from home and all its pleasures,
>   Afric's coast I left forlorn;
> To increase a stranger's treasures,
>   O'er the raging billows borne;
> Men from England bought and sold me,
>   Paid my price in paltry gold;
> But though theirs they have enroll'd me
>   Minds are never to be sold.
>
> Still in thought as free as ever,
>   What are England's rights, I ask,
> Me from my delights to sever,
>   Me to torture, me to task?
> Fleecy locks and black complexion
>   Cannot forfeit nature's claim;
> Skins may differ, but affection
>   Dwells in white and black the same.
>
> Why did all-creating Nature
>   Make the plant for which we toil?
> Sighs must fan it, tears must water,
>   Sweat of ours must dress the soil.
> Think, ye masters iron-hearted,
>   Lolling at your jovial boards;
> Think, how many backs have smarted
>   For the sweets your cane affords.

Is there, as ye sometimes tell us,
  Is there one who reigns on high?
Has he bid you buy and sell us,
  Speaking from his throne, the sky?
Ask him, if your knotted scourges,
  Fetters, blood-extorting screws,
Are the means that duty urges
  Agents of his will to use?

Hark! He answers!—Wild tornadoes
  Strewing yonder sea with wrecks,
Wasting towns, plantations, meadows,
  Are the voice with which he speaks.
He, foreseeing what vexations
  Afric's sons should undergo,
Fixed their tyrants' habitations
  Where his whirlwinds answer—No.

By our blood in Afric wasted,
  Ere our necks receiv'd the chain;
By the mis'ries which we tasted,
  Crossing in your barks the main;
By our suff'rings since ye brought us
  To the man-degrading mart;
All sustain'd by patience, taught us
  Only by a broken heart:

Deem our nation brutes no longer
  Till some reason ye shall find
Worthier of regard and stronger
  Than the colour of our kind.
Slaves of gold! whose sordid dealings
  Tarnish all your boasted pow'rs,
Prove that *you* have human feelings,
  Ere you proudly question ours.[18]

Did Charles Wesley feel that such sentiments being expressed by Cowper and others were sufficient and therefore his poetical input

---

18. The poem was written by Cowper in February 1788 and published later in *The Gentleman's Magazine*, December 1793. See Cowper, "Negro's Complaint."

was not required? This is a tantalizing question, but we shall probably never know its answer.

While Cowper speaks in specifics of the human humiliation and degradation inflicted by England's exercise of slavery, in stanza 3 of "For the Heathen" Charles simply refers to the slaves as "the heathen" and possessors of "pagan hearts" in need of transformation. While the plea for their conversion is consistent with his encounter with the black prisoner in his *MSJ* account of 1738, stanza 3 of "For the Heathen" reflects nothing of the pastoral concern encountered there: shared prayer, oneness with the black, and the administration of Holy Communion. Yet John Wesley, who after a scathing indictment of the institution of slavery in his treatise, *Thoughts Upon Slavery,* desired to express his evangelical concern for the Africans by concluding his prayer for them with stanza 3 of his brother's poem.

(3) *Court Depositions of William Floyd.* Next, we turn to the extract from the depositions in the Court of King's Bench of William Floyd, a mariner from the City of Bristol, and Little Ephraim Robin John and Ancona Robin Robin John[19] of Old Town, Old Calabar, on the coast of Africa, who became acquainted with Charles Wesley while staying for a time in Bristol.

British slave ships came frequently to Old Calabar to procure slaves and had dealings for a number of years with the Grandee, afterwards King of Old Town, Ephraim Robin John. As some locals wanted to conduct their own slave business and profit thereby, they formed the settlement of New Town. As the rivalry increased between the two factions, the British captains saw the opportunity to capitalize on the situation to their own benefit and profit and eliminate one of the parties. William Floyd explains in his deposition how the captains of a group of slave ships anchored off the coast of Old Calabar conspired to trick the leaders of Old Town to come to their ships under the guise of resolving the friction between the two towns. Their conspiracy resulted in the massacre

---

19. See Appendix A for the extract as it appeared in the *AM*. Their story has been well chronicled in Sparks, *Two Princes of Calabar.*

of some three hundred persons from Old Town who came to the ships in good faith to negotiate the resolution.

In the party from Old Town were two brothers of Ephraim Robin John, Amboe Robin John and Little Ephraim Robin John, and the latter's nephew, Ancona Robin Robin John. The people from Old Town did not suspect that the invitation from the British captains was a trap, but at the agreed-upon signal the crews of the ships began attacking those who had come aboard, as well as firing on those in the canoes. In addition, people from New Town were hidden along the shore and counter attacked, killing many who were fleeing the attack from the ships. Amboe Robin John was beheaded by the men from New Town and Little Ephraim and Ancona Robin Robin John were put in irons and, along with others who were captured, were sold into slavery.

The second part of the deposition published in *The Arminian Magazine* consists of sworn testimony of the events of the conspiracy and massacre as told by Little Ephraim Robin John and Ancona Robin Robin John. After a detailed description of the horrible events of that day, they explain that they were sold to a French doctor on the island of Dominica in the Caribbean, where they were for seven months. The captain of a ship that arrived in Dominica after hearing their story promised to take them back to Old Calabar, if they would come to the ship at night. However, he betrayed his promise and sold them to a Mr. Mitchell in Virginia, with whom they were for five years.

A Bristol Captain by the name of O'Neile, Commander of the ship *Greyhound* had two men on board who were from Old Calabar and who knew the plight of the Robin Johns. Captain O'Neile also promised to take them back to old Calabar, but told them first they would have to go to Bristol. Once again, they escaped their master and made it on to the vessel by night and were brought to Bristol. The captain also broke his promise to them and put them on a ship about to depart for Virginia in order to send them back to Mr. Mitchell.

The third extract of the deposition is once again the testimony of William Floyd, who procured a warrant from the Lord Chief

Justice Mansfield, whereby the men were brought from the ship before it could set sail for Virginia. In the court record there is a brief account of Charles Wesley's involvement with the two Africans:

> While they were at Bristol, Mr. Charles Wesley was desired to visit them. From that time they came to him every day. He taught them to read, and carefully instructed them in the principles of Christianity. They received the truth with all gladness, appeared to be deeply penetrated therewith: and after some time, desired to be baptized. There is reason to believe, they were then baptized with the Holy Ghost. After they had been in England eight or nine weeks, the people of Bristol furnished them plentifully with every thing they thought might be of use, and they set sail, with a fair wind, and abundance of prayers, for their own country.[20]

Near the African coast, however, a storm stranded the ship on a desert island, where, after a little over two weeks, they were rescued by a ship bound for Bristol. During an additional three-month sojourn there, they received further instruction in the Christian faith, reading, writing, gardening, agriculture, and the making of butter and cheese. After this stay in Bristol a second voyage was successful, and they arrived in Old Calabar.

The next three items for consideration come from the 1770s, when the Anti-Slavery movement was gaining considerable traction in England. These are: (4) personal letters to William Perronet (January 23, 1774) and Vincent Perronet (November 1, 1775), (5) a series of letters from the two slaves Ephraim Robin John and Ancona Robin Robin John, and (6) the account of these two slaves as published in *The Arminian Magazine* (1783).

Letters to William and Vincent Perronet.

(4) *Letters to William and Vincent Perronet.* There are two extant notes from the pen of Charles Wesley regarding his encounter with the slaves Ephraim Robin John and Ancona Robin Robin

20. AM 6 (1983) 211.

John. The first is a letter of January 23, 1774, written from Bristol to Mr. William Perronet. It is the postscript to the letter written on the reverse side of the letter that is of importance to this discussion. It reads:

> PS—I have had with me this month or more, two very extraordinary Scholars, and Catechumens, two African Princes carried off from Old Calabar, by a Bristol-Captain after they had seen him & his crew massacre their Brother & three hundred of their poor Countrymen.—They have been six years in Slavery; made their Escape hither; were thrown into irons, but rescued by Lord Mansfield, & [are] to be sent honourable back to their Bro[the]r, King of Calabar. This morning I baptized them.—They received both the outward visible sign, & the inward spiritual grace, in a wonderful manner & measure.[21]

The two African Princes in question, of course, are Little Ephraim Robin John and Ancona Robin Robin John. Here is Charles's record of their baptism, in which he seems to have delighted. Their correspondence with Charles Wesley is of utmost importance, since they learned English well enough to record and relate the dramatic story of their enslavement and their quest for freedom, which they ultimately achieved. Their letters to Charles have been preserved and are examined below.

The second letter by Charles Wesley with mention of the Robin Johns was addressed to Vincent Perronet and written from Bristol on November 1, 1775:[22]

> Bristol November 1, 1775.[23]
>
> Dear Sir,

---

21. See Frank Baker's transcription of this part of the letter in Baker, *Charles Wesley as Revealed by His Letters*, 122.

22. Reference number of the Methodist Archives of the John Rylands Library, Manchester, MARC, DDCW 1/65.

23. Published in the *Methodist Magazine* (1826) 33. It is also found in the Lamplough Collection.

Miss Johnson gives me an Opportunity of acknowledging y(ou)r last Favor. It brought the never-failing Blessing. You cast y[ou]r bread upon the Waters, & have found it after many days. My Father was not so happy as to *see* the Fruit of his forty years' labours at Epworth. You have both sowed & reaped. Blessed be God, who gives seed to the sower & meat to the Eater. Yours is indeed *Aquilae senectus*; & when y[ou]r work is finished, You will mount up with Eagles' Wings.

My Brother is sent back from the Gates of death in an awful Crisis of Affairs. His Example, I am persuaded, confirms Multitudes in their Loyalty; & will bring many back, who were carried away by the stream. Several other wise ends may be answered by his longer continuance; & I trust he will live to see me, & very many more of his brethren & children, gathered into the garner.

My only business now is, to end well. If the Lord renews my strength to reach London, I hope to catch the first Opportunity of visiting Shoreham, once more to receive y[ou]r Blessing and encouragement, in my last Stage. My Companion presents her warmest love & duty. Miss P[erronet] will not forget an old servant, who needs her prayers, & those of the whole church. Your Sons I bear upon my heart, as my own. May they wait upon the Lord, & renew their strength, of body and soul! I believe their latter end will be better than their beginning.

God brought us thro'[ugh] the Fire thirty years ago; and his Arm is not short'ned. Have you not faith for the poor Americans? May the two sticks become One in His hand!

My two African Children got safe home. Their Letters were suppresst at Liverpool.

If I am prospered in my journey to town, it will be another answer of y[ou]r prayers for, dearest S[i]r,

Your ever-obliged & loving,
C Wesley.

Near the end of the letter Wesley speaks of "My two African Children," who are Little Ephraim and Ancona. After their second stay in Bristol, they were finally able to travel back to their home in Old Calabar. It is this return to which Wesley refers in his letter to Vincent Perronet.

(5) *Letters from Former Slaves.* The letters of Little Ephraim and Ancona Robin Robin John to Charles Wesley[24] are of utmost importance. After being declared free through the assistance of Lord Mansfield, they remained in Bristol and the surrounding area until arrangements could be made from them to return to Old Calabar, their home in Africa. This was primarily during the last half of the year 1774. By this time Charles Wesley and his family had moved from Bristol to London, though Charles apparently made intermittent trips back to Bristol, as the New Room remained the center of Methodist activity in the west country.

How did the two Africans learn of and meet Charles Wesley? According to a letter of August 17, 1774, written in Bristol by Little Ephraim Robin John to Charles Wesley, they learned of him through Mr. Thomas Jones, who befriended them after they had been brought to Bristol by the captain who had promised to put them on another ship that would take them back to their home in Africa. Instead they were put aboard a vessel, locked in irons, and kept for eighteen days in deplorable conditions. Mr. Jones came on board the ship and requested the captain to let the two men go ashore. When he refused, Jones procured a warrant and got them off the ship. Thereafter Little Ephraim wrote to Lord Mansfield in London requesting assistance, which they ultimately received, and were freed. Mr. Jones brought the two men to his home and began to aid them with education. As they wanted to learn to read the Scriptures, the name of Charles Wesley was suggested and as Little Ephraim wrote to him, "you be better minister to teach us that we may soon come to have some knowledge of God." Ephraim further stated in this letter that it was a Mrs. Forrest who brought them to Charles Wesley.

---

24. The sources of these letters at the Methodist Archives of the John Rylands Library of the University of Manchester, UK, are listed in Appendix B. Deep gratitude is expressed to the Methodist Archives and the John Rylands Library for access to these letters.

The series of letters from Little Ephraim Robin John and Ancona Robin Robin John to Charles Wesley span the period from July to October 1774 and fill out to some extent the relationship of the two Africans to Charles Wesley and his family, as well as to John Wesley. They aid in understanding Charles's reference to Little Ephraim and Ancona as "My two African children." The letters are very important because documents written by slaves or former slaves in this period are rare. Generally speaking, their knowledge of English was very limited. Nevertheless, because of the slave trading in which the Robin Johns and their family had been engaged in Old Calabar, they had learned some English in order to communicate and conduct business. Clearly through Charles Wesley's assistance they developed better English writing and speaking skills.

It is apparent that the Robin Johns had met Charles and his family prior to the letters of July 18 and 29, 1774, the first extant letters that are preserved. The correspondence reveals that their acquaintance is indeed more than casual. In the letter of July 29 Little Ephraim and Ancona comment that they have "received with severeall good Books of Christ which Perruse as much as our weak abbilitys." Wesley is genuinely concerned that they increase their knowledge of the faith and English language through study.

In this same letter, they wish to express "our Kind Love to your wife and two Sons and Daughter," but add "admitt our Love to all our Brethren." Thus, their relationships extended beyond the bounds of the Wesley family and no doubt Charles and John sought to bring them into a wider circle of Christian community.

From the letter of Little Ephraim and Ancona dated August 5, 1775, and written from Bristol, we learn that Charles wrote letters to them as well: "Yours of the 31st July we have received and return you our most sincere thanks." There are a number of other very revealing comments in this letter. They express their concern that Charles has been ill, which they have heard from their friend Mr. Jones, and they have offered prayers for Charles's health. Little Ephraim and Ancona also indicate that they have heard John Wesley preach at the New Room in the morning and evening, after which they drank tea with Mrs. Elizabeth Johnson. John Wesley, however, "had not time to talk with us then," because "so many people follow him." Wesley tells them, however, "he will take some opportunity of doing it before he leaves Bristol and we will be glad to inform him as far as we can remember." Apparently, John had asked them to recount their experiences from capture and enslavement to freedom in England.[25]

The postscript to the letter of August 5, 1774, is a striking comment: "Yesterday we were at ye Lords table and we [are?] very comfortable in our mind—give me kind love to Miss Wesley and the two young gentlemen." Where were they at the Lord's table? In a parish church? At the New Room? They had been baptized by Charles Wesley, but were they ever confirmed in the Church of England? In another comment on the sacrament of Holy Communion from a letter of August 17, 1774, to Charles, Little Ephraim says, "Blessed be the Lord he gives us to reading his Word all the Daylong and it is very sweet to us[.] your Brother has been so kind as to talk to us and has given us the Sacrament thrice[.] I find him so good as to show me when I do wrong." It is quite clear that John and Charles do not harbor an exclusivist ecclesiology, for they have demonstrated their full intent to include Little Ephraim and Ancona in the community of the faithful, including the reception of Holy Communion.

In the postscript of his letter to William Perronet noted above Charles Wesley speaks of Little Ephraim and Ancona as "two very extraordinary Scholars, and Catechumens," and goes on to say, "This morning I baptized them.—They received both the outward visible sign, & the inward spiritual grace, in a wonderful manner & measure." There is not the slightest indication that he doubts their sincerity. A catechumen is understood as a Christian convert who is under instruction before baptism and/or one in preparation for confirmation. We have a distinct affirmation by Charles Wesley that Little Ephraim and Ancona were baptized. Whether records exist that they were confirmed at this point is not known to this author.

---

25. In a letter of August 17, 1774, they attempted to do this.

A letter dated August 27 that Charles received from Little Ephraim must have been disturbing to him. He opened the letter with the following sentence: "Dear Sir[,] one question I have to ask you before we leave England which is most on my mind that is [—] [H]ow shall I pay off good friend Mr. Jones who has been so kind in laying out so much money to seave [save] us[.] [I]f we must not sell slaves[,] I know not how we shall pay him." Jones is the one who essentially paid for the outfitting of a ship for their return voyage to Old Calabar. In a letter of Elizabeth Johnson to Charles Wesley dated August 27, 1774, she comments, "Ephraim is . . . more thoughtful and humbled. . . . Seams so full for Mr. Jones's expenses." The fact that Mr. Jones had been so kind to Little Ephraim and Ancona and had laid out so much money for their welfare and return voyage home greatly troubled Little Ephraim. The indications are that after their return to Old Calabar, they indeed did once again become involved in the trading of slaves.

A Puzzlement

Given the Wesleys' opposition to slavery and Charles Wesley's encounter with its horrors in Charleston, his intensive outreach and ministry to a condemned black in prison, and his friendship with and ministry to Little Ephraim and Ancona Robin John, why is that in his writings, with the exception of his Journal record of 1736, he does not address the evils of slavery, as does his brother John in his *Thoughts Upon Slavery*?[26]

Charles lived for many years in Bristol, one of the hotbeds of British slave trade with ships coming in and out of the landings with slaves aboard or with ships departing for Africa in order to load their vessels with slaves. One cannot imagine that he simply ignored this.

Was he unaware of William Blackstone (1723–1780), who was appointed Vinerian Professor of English Law at Oxford in 1758, and whose Oxford lectures published in 1765 set a standard for the

---

26. See the careful research on John Wesley's opposition to slavery in Brendlinger, *Social Justice through the Eyes of Wesley*.

development of British law and whose opinions on freedom and slavery became seminal for judicial interpretation of legal rights? Was Charles Wesley unaware of the case of James Somerset, who in 1771 was brought as a slave from Virginia to England and then managed to escape from his master? Shortly thereafter he was captured and forced to board a ship going to Jamaica. The following year, however, his case came before the Court of King's Bench, and after a prolonged trial, Lord Mansfield issued the judgment that regardless of whether there could be slaves in England, no master had the right to force a slave to go to another country. As a result, James Somerset was freed. While many legal aspects of the case were unclear, practically speaking Mansfield's decision helped precipitate an end to slavery in England.

One could go on and on with a variety of questions as to Charles's awareness of and response to the Abolitionist movement and the literature of the period dealing with the injustices of slavery. Why is John Wesley so clear in this matter, and Charles essentially silent? Was he simply preoccupied as a husband, father, and poet, and hence had little time for the criticism of such a dastardly institution, even though he lived at one of the thresholds of its trade, namely Bristol, for over twenty years (1749–71)? By the 1770s Charles had largely withdrawn from active engagement in the Wesleyan movement, but not from the heart of its principles, devotion to its central evangelical thrust, and its theology of inclusive grace. It is interesting that in the year 1774 the Robin Johns come to know Charles and John Wesley and write letters to Charles that John published his *Thoughts Upon Slavery*. It was probably John who asked Little Ephraim and Ancona to record the account of their enslavement, which they did in two letters dated August 17, 1774.

The Robin Johns letters most certainly emphasize that Charles never lost his pastoral concern and his ability to include those often excluded by others. His willingness to make friends of Little Ephraim and Ancona and to bring them into the embrace of his family and other Christians is overtly clear from the letters of these Africans from Old Calabar. Sharing with them in the sacraments of baptism and Holy Communion is an outward sign of what he knew the church should be—open to all, for God's grace is open to all.

It would be wrong to imply that John addressed the institution of slavery philosophically and theologically and Charles exhibited a life of pastoral and personal engagement with African slaves. Ancona Robin Robin John, in a letter dated October 10, 1774, his last before departure from England for Africa, makes the following comment about John Wesley's pastoral outreach to him and Little Ephraim in prayer: "Last night with Mr. Wesley who offerd us up in a very solemn mener to God and we humbly hope his prayer will be heard."

There is nothing in Charles Wesley's prose or poetry comparable to John's strong abolitionist statement in his treatise *Thoughts Upon Slavery*. The strongest statement from Charles is found in the words of his *MSJ* entry of 1736 in Charleston. Nevertheless, his ministry to the condemned black in prison and his friendship and diverse encounters with the Robin Johns provide a paradigm for human behavior, i.e., how human beings should relate to one another, and more specifically how Christians should relate to others regardless of racial, cultural, ethnic, and linguistic background. They must shower one another with "streams of pure celestial love."[27] This is how the earth will be made new. For Charles Wesley, of course, this transpires through the self-giving love God has revealed to all in Jesus Christ.

---

27. *UP* 1:74, stanza 5, line 5.

Chapter 4

Charles Wesley's Response to the Revolutionary War and to the American Colonies

CHARLES WESLEY WENT TO the Colony of Georgia as an ordained clergyman of the Church of England, as well as General Oglethorpe's secretary, but his brief stay was filled with turmoil and disappointment. In spite of the difficulties, there were times after his return to England that he seriously thought of returning to America. Alas, that never happened.

One must remember that he arrived in America in 1736, long before the American Revolutionary War. He became very aware of many of the domestic challenges facing the colonists, and in Boston he encountered firsthand the difficulties of not having a bishop appointed for the colonies by the Archbishop of Canterbury.

Charles Wesley's Critique of the War

For one who spent time in the colonies, it is interesting to read of Charles Wesley's strong emotional response to the independence of the American colonies after the defeat of the British. Unquestionably he was a Tory at heart and a strong supporter of the British crown. In the poem "American Independency"[1] Wesley reveals that he has followed closely the sequence of events during the Revolutionary War. For example, in lines 22 and 23: "Ask Will, why he refused to join / And save the resolute Burgoigne," refers to General William Howe's refusal to assist General John Burgoigne at the Battle of Saratoga, which evoked both praise and rebuke for his action. Then in lines 30 and 31, Charles appears to be informed about the Battle of Brandywine, a fierce battle between the forces of General George Washington and General William Howe. No doubt Charles followed carefully the published documents and public announcements about the war in the American colonies.

Lines 56 to 60 address the conclusion of the Revolutionary War with the defeat of General Charles Cornwallis in 1781 at Yorktown, Virginia.

In Wesley's view, there was never an intent to subdue the colonies. He asks, "Could we have kept America, / And forced the rebels to submit?" And answers:

> 'No: for ye ne'er intended it:
> 'Your generals ne'er in earnest fought,
> 'Or a decisive victory sought.'

In lines 75 and 76 Wesley affirms clearly what he thinks:

> And traitors force us all t'agree
> To Rebel-Independancy.

In Part II of his poem, "The American War," Wesley offers a severe critique of Great Britain and the status of the monarchy. In agony, he says:

> Your shattered State behold, and mourn
> Into a thousand parties torn;
> Your King diminished and betrayed,
> And shrunk into a Royal shade. (Lines 81–84)
> . . .
> Yet no concern they feel or pain
> For thousands, and ten thousand slain. (Lines 113–14)

---

1. See *UP* 1:102–6. Charles spells "Independancy."

After going through a litany of despair in Part III of the same poem, there is resignation in Wesley's closing lines which speak of the newly independent colonies as a "cub."

> 'And our dear Independent Cub lick
> 'Into the Shape of a Republic.' (Lines 147–48)

In Wesley's poem "American Independency," he indicates again his sincere interest in the conflict between the American colonies and Great Britain. His severe critique is more of his own nation and its policies than of the colonies and their actions. He avers that there has been a useless expenditure of funds and loss of life. Britain's own governing structure has suffered greatly, creating political turmoil.

Nevertheless, Charles's critique is too simplistic. His "veneration for the monarchy and the existing institutions of government led him to over-simplify the political issues about which he wrote."[2] He places the primary blame for the loss of the war with the Howe brothers and perhaps George Washington's prowess, as well as the British Parliament's lack of proper support of the loyalist cause in the Colonies.

No doubt the loyalists who returned to England had greatly influenced Charles. The reasons for the war and the intricacies of military maneuvering and the strategies of diverse battles were beyond Charles Wesley's interest. Furthermore, his rather blind loyalty to the crown and the Tory cause did not permit him to give due consideration to many pertinent historical facts.[3]

AMERICAN INDEPENDANCY[4]

> What harm, if ministers agree
> To rebel-independancy,
> Or British Senators consent
> To what we never can prevent?   4

---

2. Comment of Phillip O. Beale (*UP* 1:29).
3. For a better understanding of the causes of the war see Wesley, *Reflections*.
4. *MS Patriotism*, 99–104; Baker, *Rep. Verse*, 357–61.

We never can prevent it now?
But could we not? inquire of H[owe][5]
Who had the Yankies at his mercy
So oft, and drove them arsey-versey,   8
Yet still permitted to take breath,
And snatched them from the jaws of death:
Subdue them finally he coud not,
And reason good—because he woud not,   12
Who only fought for double pay,
A trust accepting—to betray.
Or let his warlike Brother[6] own
What with his Fleet he might have done,   16
Blocked all their harbours up, and seized,
Or burnt their ships, whene'er he pleased,
Their raggamuffin host compeled,
Their Chief without a stroke to yield,   20
Reduced to desperate condition,
And starved into intire submission.
Ask Will, why he refused to join
And save the resolute Burgoigne,[7]   24
Marching (his rival to betray)
Three thousand miles another way?
Right glad and happy then was he
To mock at his calamity: 28
And then with treacherous design
To spare his friends at Brandywine.[8]

5. General William Howe (1729–1814) was an early defender of the American colonies and advocated making peace with them. Nevertheless, after serving in the Revolutionary War as commander of British forces and particularly after the siege of Boston and the Battle of Bunker Hill, he no longer would defend the colonies in Parliament.

6. Admiral Lord Richard Howe (1726–1799) and Viscount Howe of Langar, was the brother of General William Howe. He also served in the Revolutionary War.

7. John Burgoyne (1722–1792), a British general, is known particularly for his defeat by American forces in the Battle of Saratoga (New York) in the campaign of 1777, during the American Revolution.

8. The Battle of Brandywine was fought between the American Continental Army of General George Washington and the British Army of General Sir William Howe on September 11, 1777, during the American Revolutionary War (1775–1783).

Or let Monsieur sincerely say
Coud we have kept America, 32
And forced the rebels to submit—
'No: for ye ne'er intended it:
'Your generals ne'er in earnest fought,
'Or a decisive victory sought; 36
'To trust their friends with arms afraid,
'Lest Loyalists themselves should aid,
'And crush their foes, and mar the plots
'Of spurious, English Patriots.' 40
Our Patriots here, a restless Party,
For their Allies abroad so hearty,
Might safely promise and foretell
America invincible, 44
While all in the conspiracy
Determin'd—It shall never be
That Britain shoud obtain her ends
And triumph o'er Rebellion's friends. 48
Oft when the Cause appeared as lost
And ready to give up the ghost,
By some political manouvre
They helped their Partners to recover, 52
The last, expiring spark of war
Revived, and snatched them from despair:
Till headlong and precipitate
C[ornwalli]s[9] rushed upon his fate: 56
Yielding at once without a stroke,
And passing, tame, beneath the yoke,
He *begd* the haughty Foe to spare
His sutlers, and his tools of war, 60
But left the Loyalists to feel
The mercy of those Fiends from hell.
Woud faction's sons neglect th'occasion
Of subjecting both King and nation? 64
Furious they rise with one consent,
And seize the helm of government;

---

9. In 1781, British General Charles Cornwallis (1738–1805) surrendered ca. eight thousand British troops and seamen to a French and American force at Yorktown, Virginia, which ended the American Revolution.

They vote, of sovereign power possest,
The ruinous war at once supprest, 68
And all who dare their plans oppose
Declare their King's and Country's foes:
Loyalists must the strife give o'er,
The soldiers must contend no more, 72
But from America withdraw,
And congress give to Britain law,
And traitors force us all t'agree
To Rebel-Independency. 76

PART II

O what a scene before us lies,
When Britons use their open eyes!
Britons, employ them now and see
Your weak, dismembered Monarchy, 80
Your shattered State behold, and mourn
Into a thousand parties torn;
Your King diminished and betrayed,
And shrunk into a Royal shade; 84
Your Country sold by his own sons,[10]
And dying with convulsive groans;
Your brethren for their loyal zeal
Abandoned to the murtherer's will; 88
Your Provinces Rebellion's prey,
Renounced, and vilely cast away
(Kingdoms that countless millions cost)
And public Faith for ever lost! 92
See the brave men of British race,
Our nation's glory, and disgrace,
Commanded to stand forth in fight,
T'assert their King's and Country's Right, 96
Promised by both protection sure,
And in our plighted faith secure;
Yet while to Us for help they look,
Disowned, disfranchised, and forsook, 100
Their Country's gratitude to prove,
And perish for their faithful love,

---

10. Charles Wesley's daughter Sally replaces "his own" with "Briton's."

To spread thro' earth the British name,
And brand us with eternal shame.	104
See, how the bold, rapacious Great
Their Rivals, and their King intreat!
They strip him of his wealth and power,
That patriots may both devour,	108
They load him with indignities,
And threaten all his realms to seize,
Who gave the larger half away
In spite, and lost America.	112
Yet no concern they feel or pain
For thousands, and ten thousand slain,
Yet no remorse the ruffians know
For millions plunged in hopeless woe:	116
The ruffians, wallowing in excess,
And glorying in their wickedness,
By no account hereafter awd,
Injoy the wrath, and curse of God.	120

PART III

How strange a sight at court appears!
A Congress of first ministers,
Each other who in pieces tear,
Ingaged in an intestin war,	124
And to the brink of ruin bring
Themselves, their Country, and their King,
Furious the shattered helm to seize
And rule their Ruler as they please.	128
He hears their insolent demands,
'Give up your power into our hands:
'The Power executive are we
'And absolute is our decree:	132
'Either from us receive the law,
'Or, Sire, to Hanover withdraw,
'Tamely submit to Abdication
'(Unless you chuse Decapitation)	136
'And vacant leave the throne, nor fear
'We soon shall find a Successor.
'Either the Youth so wise and good,
'Or One of Charles's spurious brood,	140

'Perhaps we may permit a while
'To bear, for form, the Regal style,
'Till we have perfected our Plan
'As high and mighty States to reign,   144
'And following Congress's example
'On Kings and Monarchy to trample
'And our dear Independent Cub lick
'Into the Shape of a Republic.'   148

Charles Wesley's Critique of the Colonies

Along with a harsh critique of the British Generals Richard and William Howe for their handling of the war with the colonies, Wesley also has some very strong language for the colonies themselves, though he expresses tremendous support for the British loyalists left in the colonies and those who had returned to England. The colonies are described as useless.

> The people swimming with the tide,
> And strenuous on the rebels' side,
>   Rejoiced in their success
> (Rais'd from the dust to sovereign sway;)
> And praised the men who cast away
>   Our useless colonies.[11]

He also cannot resist mentioning slavery in the colonies, which he experienced first hand in Charleston before his return to England and would oppose for the rest of his life. In a poem titled "II. Written in October 1783 for the Loyal Americans" he wrote:

> The men who dared their loyal love,
> Their sworn fidelity approve,
>   Their king and country own,
> Where treason and rebellion reign
> And perjured slaves their sway maintain
>   And Satan *keeps* his throne.[12]

---

11. From "The Testimony of the American Loyalists, 1783" (*UP* 1:128).
12. *UP* 1:137.

In Charles's poem "The Patriot's Address" one finds again high praise for those who remained loyal to the British crown[13] and nation. The loyalists he claims are "Anxious, and full of loyal zeal," but he has no praise for the colonies. He queries:

> Why should we now renounce our case
> For a few paultry colonies?

Then he continues quite sarcastically:

> Why vindicate our Monarch's right,
> Or for the Constitution fight,
> For king and country what care we,
> For George, or his Supremacy?
> For Loyalists, or their distresses?
> Our care is—to secure our places,
> The brave Americans to crown,
> And turn this kingdom upside down.

He then becomes quite solemn and serious as he considers the importance of peace:

> Our first resolve we first declare
> To end at once this ruinous war:
> But if both sides refuse to bend
> How should the quarrel have an end?
> Then let us beg, or buy a peace,
> The high and mighty States confess,
> Allow them to be independent—
> And thus we make a glorious end on't![14]

Charles Wesley's long, epic poem of over six-hundred lines, "The American War," is laced with merciless criticism of the Howe brothers as leaders of the British forces. While Wesley shows that he followed quite seriously the events of the Revolutionary War, his own biases surface on every page of the poem. Nor does he have any complimentary words for George Washington.

---

13. Charles's loyalty to the British monarchy is reflected in a number of Charles's poems dedicated to King George the Third.

14. *UP* 1:149.

> Washington, at his friend's devotion
> And near to watch his every motion,
> A ragged Regiment employs
> (To rob or starve their only choice),
> And daily sends them forth to plunder
> And keep the harass'd country under,
> Make every loyalist their prey,
> Imprison, brand, and burn, and slay;
> Beseige and cut the General short,
> Nine months shut up within his fort.
>
> . . .
>
> As a gaunt wolf, by day and night
> To keep the country in a fright,
> To whip or hang the countrymen,
> And then slink back into his den.[15]

Given the extent of Charles Wesley's vast creative corpus, it is clear that after his return to England and his conversion experience of 1738, he had a singular purpose: to share the Gospel as revealed in the Scriptures, and in and through the Church to develop the nurture of a daily spiritual walk with God. He turns his primary interest to encouraging and developing a way of spirituality, as his lyrical composition clearly shows. After his marriage in 1749, it is also evident that much of his devotion is to his wife and children. His poetry for the next decades reflects the importance of these concerns, spirituality and family, as his interest in the colonies tends to wane.

---

15. *UP* 1:53–54.

Appendix A

List of the Letters from Ancona Robin Robin John and Ephraim Robin John to Charles Wesley and from Elizabeth Johnson regarding these two former African slaves

Methodist Archives

JRL Number	Call Number	Author	Date of Work
0700530cb	DDCW 2/3	Ancona Robin Robin John	1774-08-08
0700531cb	DDCW 2/3	Ancona Robin Robin John	1774-08-08
0700532cb	DDCW 2/4	Ancona Robin Robin John	1774-08-17
0700533cb	DDCW 2/4	Ancona Robin Robin John	1774-08-17
0700534cb	DDCW 2/4	Ancona Robin Robin John	1774-08-17
0700535cb	DDCW 2/5	Ephraim Robin John	1774-08-17
0700536cb	DDCW 2/5	Ephraim Robin John	1774-08-17
0700537cb	DDCW 2/5	Ephraim Robin John	1774-08-17

APPENDIX A: LETTERS

JRL Number	Call Number	Author	Date of Work
0700538cb	DDCW 2/6	Ancona Robin & Ephraim Robin John	1774-02-18
0700539cb	DDCW 2/7	Ancona Robin & Ephraim Robin John	1774-02-24
0700540cb	DDCW 2/9	E. Johnson & Ephraim Robin John	1774-08-27
0700541cb	DDCW 2/9	E. Johnson & Ephraim Robin John	1774-08-28
0700542cb	DDCW 2/10	Ephraim Robin John	1774-09-26
0700543cb	DDCW 2/10	Ephraim Robin John	1774-09-26
0700544cb	DDCW 2/11	Ephraim Robin John	1774-10-10
0700545cb	DDCW 2/11	Ephraim Robin John	1774-10-10
0700546cb	DDCW 2/12	Ephraim Robin John & Ancona Robin Robin John	1774

JRL = John Rylands Library

Methodist Archives = The Methodist Archives located at the John Rylands Library of the University of Manchester, UK.

Appendix B

An Extract from the Depositions of William Floyd, of the City of Bristol, Mariner, and Little Ephraim Robin John, and Ancona Robin Robin John, of Old Town, Old Calabar, on the Coast of Africa.[1]

In the Court of King's-Bench

WILLIAM FLOYD MAKETH OATH, That he hath been employed in the African trade, as Mate and Master of a vessel, about twenty years: that in the year 1767, he was Chief Mate of the Merchant Ship, called the *Indian Queen*, John L———tt, Master: that in that year the said ship was in the river of Old Calabar, with the *Duke of York*, Capt. James Beven; the *Nancy*, Capt. M———ll; the *Concord*, Capt. ———, all of Bristol: the *Edgar*, Capt. A. L———, of Liverpool, and a ship belonging to London, Capt. Parks: that a quarrel having for some time subsisted between the inhabitants of Old Town, Old Calabar, and those of New Town, Old Calabar: the principal inhabitants of Old Town, were invited on board the said ships by the several Captains, who promised to make an end of the quarrel between them and their neighbours: that trusting in this promise, between three and four hundred of them, in ten

1. *AM* (1783) 98-99.

APPENDIX B: THE DEPOSITIONS OF WILLIAM FLOYD

canoes, came, first on the long side of the *Indian Queen*, and afterwards went on board the *Edgar*, leaving three or four of their people on board the *Indian Queen*, one of whom was Amboe Robin John, brother of Ephraim Robin John, then a Grandee, afterwards the King of Old Town: that the next morning there were on board the *Indian Queen*, two other persons, who came on the same invitation, Little Ephraim Robin John, another brother of the said Grandee, and Ancona Robin Robin John, the nephew. That the same morning, Amboe Robin John, Litte Ephraim, and Ancona, were sent by Capt. Beven, with others belonging to their canoe, with a Letter on board the *Edgar*: that mean time canoes going from the *Edgar*, carried many of the inhabitants from Old Town and distributed them on board the other ships: that the same morning Capt. L. gave this deponent orders, that as soon as he saw a jack at the mizen top mast head, he should seize all the people of Old Town that were on board: that having for some time waited the signal, he heard and saw a firing of small arms and wall-pieces from the *Duke of York*, into a canoe lying alongside her, belonging to Amboe, Little Ephraim, and Ancona: that presently after he saw the canoe sink, and several of the people swimming in the water, most of whom were either killed, or seized and carried on board the said ship: that immediately upon the said firing, all the other ships in the river (except the *Edgar* and the *Concord*) began to fire on the other canoes, and to seize the men who were not killed: that during this firing, many of the inhabitants of New Town, who had lain concealed on the shore, began to pursue such as had escaped by swimming; and several from the ships joined them in the pursuit: that afterwards he saw many dead bodies in the river, and on the sands: that about three hundred (many of them principal men of the place) were either killed or made slaves of: that Amboe Robin John was delivered by Capt. Beven, to the inhabitants of New Town, one of whom immediately struck off his head, along-side of the ship: and that many others were carried by the *Duke of York* and the other ships, and sold for slaves in the plantations of America.

Selected Bibliography

Baker, Frank. *Charles Wesley as Revealed by His Letters*. London: Epworth, 1948.
Brendlinger, Irv A. *Social Justice through the Eyes of Wesley: John Wesley's Theological Challenge to Slavery*. Ontario, Canada: Joshua, 2006.
Classified Digest of the Records of the Society for the Propagation of the Gospel in Foreign Parts 1701–1892. London: Society's Office, 1893.
Coleman, Kenneth, ed. *A History of Georgia*. 2nd ed. Athens: University of Georgia, 1991.
Cowper, William. "The Negro's Complaint." *The Gentleman's Magazine*, December 1793. *Luminarium: Anthology of English Literature*. Online. http://www.luminarium.org/eightlit/cowper/negroscomplaint.htm.
Danker, Ryan N. "The Younger Brother Unveiled: Charles Wesley and Anglicanism in Colonial Boston." *Methodist Review* 6 (2014) 1–26.
Foote, H. W. *Annals of King's Chapel from the Puritan Age of New England to the Present Day*. 2 vols. Boston: Little, Brown, and Co., 1882.
Fryer, Peter. *Staying Power: The History of Black People in Britain*. London: Pluto, 1984.
Gerzina, Gretchen. *Black England: Life before Emancipation*. London: John Murray, 1995.
Heitzenrater, Richard P. "Early Sermons of John and Charles Wesley." In *Mirror and Memory: Reflections on Early Methodism*, 150–61. Nashville: Kingswood, 1989.
———. "Charles Wesley and James Oglethorpe in Georgia," *PCWS* 13 (2009) 19–33.

SELECTED BIBLIOGRAPHY

Heitzenrater, Richard P., and Randy L. Maddox, eds. *The Journal Letters and Related Biographical Items of the Rev. Charles Wesley, MA*. Nashville: Kingswood, 2018.

———. *Letters I (1721–1739)*. Vol. 25 of *The Works of John Wesley*. Nashville: Abingdon, 1987.

Heitzenrater, Richard P., and W. R. Ward, eds. *Journals and Diaries I (1735–1738)*. Vol. 18 of *The Works of John Wesley*. Nashville: Abingdon, 1988.

Hoole, Elijah. *Oglethorpe and the Wesleys in America*. London: R. Needham, 1863.

Jackson, Thomas, ed. *The Journal of Charles Wesley*. 2 Vols. London: Mason, 1849.

Kimbrough, S T, Jr. "Charles Wesley in Boston." *Methodist History* 45 (2007) 111–33.

———. "Charles Wesley in Georgia." *Methodist History* 45 (2007) 88–99.

Kimbrough, S T, Jr., and Oliver A. Beckerlegge, eds. *The Unpublished Poetry of Charles Wesley*. 3 vols. 1988. Nashville: Kingswood, 1992.

Kimbrough, S T, Jr., and Kenneth G. C. Newport, eds. *The Manuscript Journal of The Reverend Charles Wesley, MA*. 2 vols. Nashville: Kingswood, 2008.

Marsch, Angelika. *Die Salzburger Emigranten in Bildern*. 2nd ed. Weissenhorn: Anton H. Konrad Verlag, 1979.

McIlvenna, Noeleen. *The Short Life of Free Georgia*. Chapel Hill: University of North Carolina, 2015.

Moore, Henry. *The Life of the Rev. John Wesley*. 2 Vols. London: John Kershaw, 1824.

Newport, Kenneth G. C. *The Sermons of Charles Wesley*. Oxford: Oxford University, 2001.

Osborn, George, ed. *The Poetical Works of John and Charles Wesley*. 13 Vols. London: Methodist Conference, 1868–1872.

Reese, Trevor Richard. *Colonial Georgia: A Study in British Imperial Policy in the Eighteenth Century*. Athens: University of Georgia, 1963.

Schmidt, Martin. *John Wesley: A Theological Biography*. Translated by Norman Goldhawk. 3 vols. Nashville: Abingdon, 1962–1973.

Shipton, Clifford Kenyon, ed. *Sibley's Harvard Graduates*. Vol. 4. Cambridge, MA: Harvard University Press, 1933.

Spalding, Phinizy. *Oglethorpe in America*. Chicago: University of Chicago Press, 1977.

Sparks, Randy J. *The Two Princes of Calabar: An Eighteenth Century Atlantic Odyssey*. Cambridge, MA: Harvard University Press, 2004.

Swanton, John R. *The Indian Tribes of North America*. Bureau of American Ethnology Bulletin 145. Washington, DC: US Government Printing Office, 1953.

Telford, John, ed. *The Journal of Charles Wesley*. London: Hazell, Watson, and Viney, 1910.

SELECTED BIBLIOGRAPHY

Tyng, Dudly. *Massachusetts Episcopalians 1607–1957*. Pascoag, RI: Delmo, 1957.
Watts, Isaac. *Horae Lyricae*. London: Humfreys, 1709.
———. *Hymns and Spiritual Songs*. London: Humfreys, 1707.
Wesley, Charles. *Hymns of Intercession for All Mankind*. Bristol: Farley, 1758.
Wesley, John. *Reflections on the Rise and Progress of the American Rebellion*. London: J. Paramore, 1780.
Wesley, Samuel. *Poems on Several Occasions*. London: E. Say, 1736.
White, George, ed. *Historical Collections of Georgia*. New York: Pudney & Russell, 1855.

Index of Personal Names

Appee, Peter, 4, 16, 42, 63–64, 74
Ayilón, Vásquez de, xvi

Beale, Phillip, 108
Belcher, Andrew, 60
Belcher, Jonathan, 60, 75, 79
Blackstone, William, 103
Bovey, Miss [Rebecca], 16, 35, 63
Brig, Mr., 61–62
Broughton, Mr. [Thomas], 87, 88
Burgoigne, John, 107, 109

Caesar, Augustus, 13
Causton, Thomas, 3, 40
Checkley, John, 52, 56–61, 73
Colwell, Mrs., 40
Cornish, John, 3, 74
Cornwallis, Charles, 107, 110n9,
Cowper, William, 93–95
Curnock, Nehemiah, xix, 17
Cutler, John, 55
Cutler, Timothy, 50–51, 54–56,
    60–62, 65–67, 77

Davenport, Addington, 62–63, 66, 80
Davison, Samuel (constable), 21, 36

Delamotte, Charles, 4, 35–36, 45
Delegall, Ensign, 38
Dempsey, Captain, 39
Dison, Mr., 40
Drake, Sir Francis, 41

Ferguson,[William] Captain, 39
Floyd, William, vi, 84, 95–96,
    119–20
Forrest, Mrs., 100
Frazer, W[illiam], 33, 40

Gardner, Dr., 65
Gascoin, 41
George II, King, xvi, 60
George III, King, 114n13
Germain, Mr. [Michael], 39
Germain, Mrs. [Michael], 6–8, 39
Gibbons, Dr., 65
Greaves (Graves), Dr. [Thomas], 64,
    68, 71
Green, Bishop, 55
Greenaway, Mr., 87

Hastings, Lady Margaret, 38
Hawkins, Dr. Thomas, 20–21, 36–38

125

INDEX OF PERSONAL NAMES

Hawkins, Mrs. Thomas (Beata), 2, 6, 10, 13, 17–21, 22n50, 23–29, 32, 36–38, 40, 44–45
Hermsdorf, Captain Johann Christian Adolf von, 20, 29, 37
Hill, Mr., 82–83
Hird, Mark, 37
Hird, Mrs. Grace, 37
Hird, Thomas, 17, 21
Homer, 15, 44
Hoole, Elijah, xix, 14, 17, 19, 24–28
Horace, 15, 44
Horton, Mr. William, 33, 37, 39
Howe, Richard, xxi, 78, 109n6, 113–14
Howe, William, xxi, 78, 107–8, 109n5n6n8, 113–14
Hudson, Mr., 87–88
Huntingdon, Countess Selina, 38
Hutchinson, Mr., 40
Hutton, James, 86

Ignatio, Don, 33, 39
Indivine, Captain, 42, 64, 70
Ingham, Benjamin, 4, 13, 22, 35, 37–38, 45

Jackson, Thomas, 1n1, 11–12, 17–18, 22
Johnson, Elizabeth, vi, 99, 101, 103, 117–18
Jones, Thomas, 100–101, 103

Lamberti, Don Pedro de, 33, 39
Lassel [Lascelles], Mr. [Henry, Jr.], 40
Laserre,[1] Mr., 73, 82–83
Lawley, Mr. [Richard], 38
Lawley, Mrs. [Anne], 38
Lynch, Colonel, 82–83

Macintosh, [John Mohr] Captain, 39

Mansfield, Lord William Murray, 97–98, 100, 104
Manuel, Don, 39
Mather, Cotton, 51
Miller, Ebenezer, 61, 66–67
Mitchell, Mr., 96
Moore, Lieutenant, 39
Mouse, Mrs. [Lucy], 40
Musgrove, John, xvi

Newington, Mr., 86–88
Newton, John, 93
Nitschmann, Bishop David, 3

Oglethorpe, James, v, xvn1, xvi–xviii, xx, 1–6, 8–10, 13–14, 17–19, 23–41, 43–47, 52–53, 56, 63–64, 73–75, 106
O'Neile, Captain, 96

Parker, Mr. [Henry], 40
Pascal, Blaise, 68
Perronet, Vincent, xx, 85, 97–98, 100
Perronet, William, xx, 85, 97–98, 102
Perkins, Mrs., 40
Plasted, Mr., 65, 67
Plasted, Mrs., 65, 67
Pohoia, Chief of the Floridas, 33, 41
Price, Elizabeth, 54, 61–62, 67
Price, Roger, 50, 54–55, 62–63, 65, 67, 69–70, 75–76
Price, William, 54
Prince, Thomas, 59n17

Richards, Major, 33, 39–40
Robin John, Amboe, 96, 120
Robin John, Ancona Robin, vi, xiii, xxi, 84–85, 95–105, 117–20
Robin John, Ephraim (Grandee), 95, 120

---

1. Charles Wesley spells Lasserre.

126

INDEX OF PERSONAL NAMES

Robin John, Little Ephraim, vi, xiii, xxi, 84–85, 95–105, 117–20
Robinson, Mrs., 40

Shakespeare, William, 16, 44
Somerset, James, 104
Soto, Hernan de, xv
Sparks, Mr., 86–87
Star, Mr., 82–83

Tackner, Mr. [Ambrose], 40
Telford, John, xix, 1n1, 5, 11–12, 17, 19–21, 23–24, 26–29,
Thomas, Captain, 24
Tomo Chachi (Tomochichi), Chief of the Yamacraw tribe, xvi, 3, 40
Towers, Thomas, 40

Vernon, James, 40
Virgil, 14, 44

Walpole, Sir Robert, 41
Washington, George, 107–8, 109n8, 114–15
Washington, Mr. [Henry], 87
Welch, Anne, 2, 6, 10, 13, 17–30, 32, 38, 44–45
Welch, John, 21, 24, 38
Wesley, John, viii, xi, xvii, 2–3, 18, 24, 26–27, 30–31, 35, 37–40, 43, 63, 91, 95, 101, 104–5
Wesley, Samuel, Jr., 16
Wesley, Samuel, Sr., 86n9
Wesley, Sarah (Sally). Jr., 111
Wesley, Sarah (Sally), Sr., viii
Whitefield, George, 46–47, 76–77, 84
Williams, Mrs. Nathaniel, 58, 65
Williams, Nathaniel, ix, 58–59, 65, 79
Woodward, Henry, xvi

Zouberbuhler, Mr., 82–83

Index of Place Names

Amelia Island, 33

Boston, xviii–xx, 43, 46, 48, 50,
  52–54, 56–61, 63–67, 69–72,
  75–80, 106
Boston Long Wharf, 43, 49
Braintree, 61–62, 67
Bristol (England), vi, ix, xxi, 84–85,
  95–104, 119

Cambridge (Massachusetts), 60–62,
  67
Cape Cod, 43
Charleston (Charlestown), vi, ix,
  xviii, xx, 35–38, 41–43, 46,
  52, 55, 81–84, 88, 103, 105,
  113
Cumberland Island, 33

Fort Frederica, 3–6, 9, 15, 31, 33–38,
  52, 73
Fort St. Andrews, 33
Fort St. George, 33, 37

Gravesend, xvi, 2–3

Hyde Park (England), 87n10

Jamaica, 104
Jekyll's Island, 33
Jekyll's Sound, 39

London, vii, xvi, 30, 50, 56, 65, 67,
  75, 87n10, 99–100, 119

New Town (Old Calabar), 95–96,
  119–20
Newgate (prison, England), 85–86

Old Calabar (Coast of Africa), vi,
  84, 95–98, 100–101, 103–4,
  119–20
Old Town (Old Calabar), vi, 84,
  95–96, 119
Oxford (England), viii, 2, 37, 52, 54,
  61–62, 70, 80, 103

Quincy, 61

Salzburg, 37
Saratoga (New York), 107, 109n7

129

INDEX OF PLACE NAMES

Savannah (Georgia), v, xvi, 3–5, 7,
    34–36, 38, 40, 45
Scituate, 62
Shoreham (England), 99
South Braintree, 61
St. Augustine, 33–34, 37, 39–40
St. Catherine's Island, xv
St. George's Point, 33, 41
St. Simon's Island, xviii, 2, 4, 52
Stratford, (Connecticut), 55

Thunderbolt, 35
Tibey Island, xvii
Tiverton, 16, 74
Tyburn, Middlesex (England), 87

Virginia, 96–97, 104, 107, 110n9

Yorkshire, 38
Yorktown (Virginia), 107, 110n9

www.ingramcontent.com/pod-product-compliance
Lightning Source LLC
Chambersburg PA
CBHW051943160426
43198CB00013B/2273